Walks
on the
Isle of Skye

by

Mary Welsh

Illustrated by Margaret Clarke
and David Macaulay
with maps by Don Clarke

Front cover illustration by David Macaulay

Westmorland Gazette, Kendal, Cumbria

First published 1990

ISBN 0 902272 83 7

© Westmorland Gazette, 1990
Reprinted 1995

Published by
Westmorland Gazette
22 Stricklandgate, Kendal, Cumbria

Printed by
Titus Wilson & Son Ltd, Kendal, Cumbria

Preface

In this book I have described 37 walks in all parts of the lovely island of Skye – a favourite part of Scotland to which I have returned again and again, always with intense pleasure, over the years.

I have written about the birds, animal life and plants most likely to be seen and the terrain to be covered. The book is for those who wish to leave the road and set off into the hills and mountains, walk over the moorland, tramp through quiet woodland or dawdle along the lovely coastline.

Remember as you prepare to walk that the sun does not always shine and that you must take waterproofs. For safety wear walking boots, and for longer walks take extra clothing and sufficient food and drink.

My thanks go to my family and friends, who walked with me and encouraged me on my way; to Don and Margaret Clarke, who did the maps and some of the drawings; to David Macaulay, who drew the other pictures and designed the cover, and finally to my dog, Cammy, who covered every mile with me.

Good walking!

Map of Skye

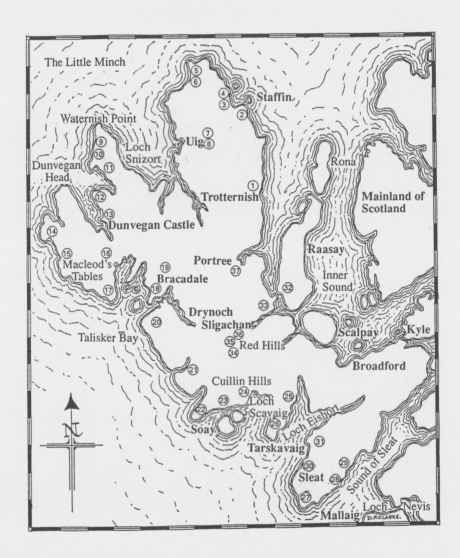

The Little Minch

5
6
4
3
Staffin
2

Waternish Point

7
Uig 8
9
Loch
10
Snizort
11
Dunvegan
Head
12
13
Dunvegan Castle

Rona

Trotternish

Mainland of
Scotland

Raasay

1

15
Macleod's
Tables
16
Portree
19
Bracadale
37
Inner
Sound
17
18
32

Drynoch
Sligachan
33
20
23
Talisker Bay
36
35
Red Hills
34
Scalpay
Kyle

Broadford

21

Cuillin Hills
24
23
Loch
25
22
Scavaig
26
Loch Eishort
31
Soay

N

Tarskavaig
30
29
Sleat
28
27
Mallaig
Loch
Nevis
Sound of Sleat

D.F.CLARKE.

Contents

Contents (continued)

1. Walk to The Storr including the Old Man

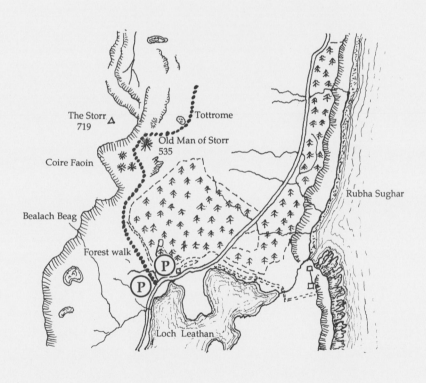

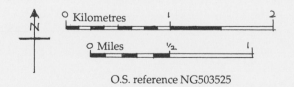

O.S. reference NG503525

Leave Portree by the A855. After six miles watch for the magic moment when first Loch Fada and then Loch Leathan come into view, with the Old Man of Storr and one of its satellites high up on the skyline above. Park in the Forestry Commission car park. Take the path into the forest leading from the northern corner. Pass through rides where goldcrests call and heather and scabious colour the way.

Goldcrests

After heavy rain, however, the forest path sometimes becomes impassable and the forest is closed. If it is, turn and drive back a quarter of a mile to a large lay-by with room for a dozen or so cars on the Storr ridge side of the road. Cross the wire fence by a stile and walk up the path ahead.

The narrow path passes through damp moorland where the delicate and lovely grass of parnassus grows. Continue through the bracken beside a narrow racing burn. This has to be crossed and its volume will dictate how you get over it – maybe a stride will suffice. Continue up the steep hill slope, walking between the forest fence and a derelict drystone wall. This path continues climbing steadily for over half a mile. Follow the fence as it turns to the right above the large plantation of conifers. Ahead lies a fence that stretches from the forest fence to the giant buttress at the start of the range of mountains. Cross this and join the distinct path that has passed through the forest from the car park.

Grass of parnassus

This narrow path ascends to the tortured shapes above, and progress up the very steep slope is helped by footprint steps and large zig-zags. Finally the path levels out and turns to the right, passing between two monstrous, jagged, rough-sided tors. From now on you can choose your path for there are many and all are good and safe. Wander at will through this moon landscape, where no rock has been softened by nature or by man, and let your imagination have free rein. Pass through the first hollow, with its various shaped and angled pinnacles leaning 'crazily' about it. Proceed through the next, much deeper, hollow, which again is guarded about its rim by twisted, pitted bastions of basalt.

The Storr and Loch Fada

All paths seem to lead to the bottom of the Old Man, a huge pear-shaped leaning pillar of rock, 160 feet in height, which is recessed at its base. Climb up the mound of earth and rock on which the Old Man appears to balance so precariously and scramble around its base. Splendid views of the lochs below, with Raasay, Rona and the mainland mountains beyond, stretch into the misty distance. Picnic in the hollow below the mound, out of the wind.

Running along behind these weird and fantastic pinnacles are the buttresses of the Storr ridge, the highest reaching 3,000 feet above sea level. This formidable wall of rock, with its stone-floored gullies and its blasted and riven surface, overtops the jagged obelisks below. It is a fearsome place, one that sets one's senses tingling, until a soft mist drifts in from the sea and slowly descends lower and lower over the buttresses, hiding all the roughness. Walk on along the path above a tiny lochan and view the Old Man from the other side.

Among the pinnacles and tors, the earth is littered with boulders and some scree but between these the grass is soft to walk on. Lady's mantle and alpine lady's mantle grow in soft cushions. Wild thyme, eyebright, tormentil, felwort and alpine scurvy grass grow on the slopes and in the rocky crevices rose-root flourishes.

The peace of these hollows in the hills is profound but occasionally a deep croak echoing off the buttresses reminds you that you are not alone; you are sharing it with the ravens.

This glorious three-mile walk could take you as much as four hours.

3 miles
4 hours

Walk 2

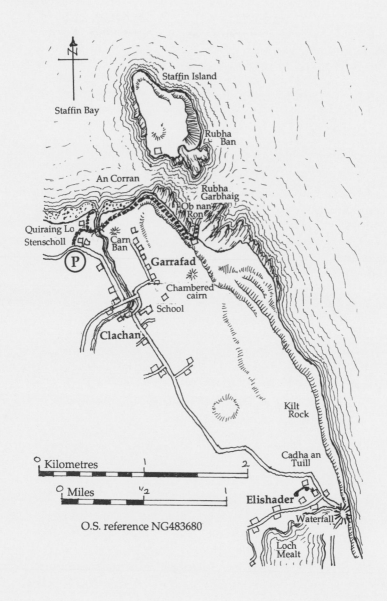

Staffin Island

Staffin Bay

Rubha Ban

An Corran

Rubha Garbhaig

Ob nan Ron

Quiraing Lo
Stenscholl

Carn Ban

P

Garrafad

Chambered cairn

School

Clachan

Kilt Rock

Kilometres

Cadha an Tuill

Miles

Elishader

Waterfall

Loch Mealt

O.S. reference NG483680

2. Walk in Staffin Bay (the place of staff-like pillars)

Drive along the A855, pausing in the well-signposted car park to view the Mealt Falls and the Kilt Rock. The magnificent waterfall, formed from the waters of Loch Mealt, drops 300 feet into the sea, foaming and raging. Beyond the falls stands the curious rock formation of columnar basalt that looks like organ pipes or the pleats of a kilt – hence its name. Fulmars settle on the crevices and circle around the cliff face before returning to their special niches. Continue northwards for two-and-a-quarter miles, parking in the lay-by beneath the war memorial at Stenscholl (stone slope). Walk down the narrow lane signposted Staffin Slip, past alders heavy with nuts. Cattle shelter here from the wind that can sometimes roar across the island. The lane is bordered with summer flowers – hardheads, wild mint, purple loosestrife, sneezewort yarrow, clover and meadow sweet.

Wild mint

If you continue along the lane, past Quiraing Lodge, you reach a gate which gives access to the shore. Oystercatchers pipe. Grass and eyebright continue to the edge of the beach, composed here of huge round pebbles. Follow the little path as it curves northwards along the shore.

Purple loosestrife

When you have walked as far as you wish, return to the gate, walk a few yards along the lane and follow it as it swings to the left. It passes beneath a small cliff where ancient alders grow. Through the trees flit blue tits, great tits, chaffinches, robins, blackbirds and wrens. Swallows wheel and dive overhead enjoying the insects – both hunters and hunted protected from the gales by the cliff and its trees. Below the alders, ferns and flowers flourish.

Cross the wooden bridge over the surging Stenscholl River. As it races through a narrow gap in the rocks and then over a weir, its foam is slashed with peat stain. Turn left over the bridge and walk along beside the burn. Just where the river enters the sea a pair of dippers and one of their brood feed in the fast-flowing water. They run into the water, sometimes submerging totally. Then they stand on rocks, the brilliant white bibs of the adults and the yellowy breast patch of the youngster revealing their presence among the dark boulders of the beach.

Walk on along the soft, springy turf, where sheep graze, to a soft black sandy beach with a good view of Staffin Island. Walk up a narrow path to rejoin the road, turn left and continue along the road, which now hugs the sheer basalt cliffs. Pied wagtails race across the turf and a great northern diver hunts for fish just off the shore. The road ends at a small slipway – Ob nan Ron.

Great northern diver

On your return, walk back along the road, over the bridge and through the alders. Continue along the lane, pausing by a

13

gap in the trees, and look across the crofters' pastures where oats and hay grow and cattle graze. Look over the lovely Staffin Bay to Flodigarry Island, hilly and grassy, its shores a mass of white breakers as the wind tosses the waves against its cliffs. Dominating this scene of beauty is the huge brooding presence of Quiraing, a black mass of mountain. The detail of its gullies, ridges, pinnacles and buttresses is lost to sight because of the darkness of the stormy sky. Some of its sinister blackness is softened by wisps of cloud that tangle with The Needle and move down onto The Table.

This delightful short walk is just right for one of those days when everywhere else on Skye seems battered by storm force winds.

2 miles
2 hours

3. Walk through the Quiraing (stronghold or ringed fence)

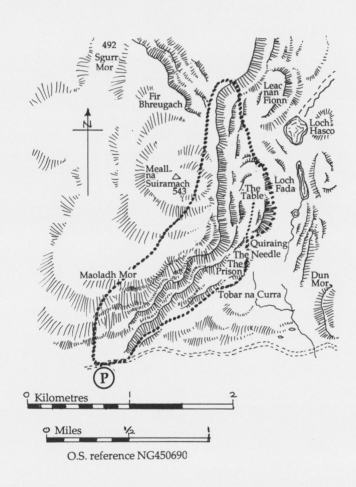

O.S. reference NG450690

Drive along the single-track road that crosses the pass between Staffin and Uig (bay) and park in the large lay-by at the highest point. Before you set off on this walk, memorise the steep slopes opposite so that on your return you can come down safely, avoiding the cliffs to your right.

Follow the wide, well-used track that skirts a picnic table on a rocky outcrop immediately in front of you. Enjoy the marvellous views of Staffin Bay, the Island of Rona and the mountains of Wester Ross. Look down to the hairpin bends on the pass, and beyond to the lochans and the mountain range.

Ahead lie the tortured rocks, pinnacles and cliffs of basalt that make up the area known as Quiraing. Through this lunar-like landscape the path continues. Wheatears and meadow pipits flit ahead. Heather and grass cover the slopes and among these grow wild strawberry and alpine lady's mantle. A ravine across the path at first sight seems difficult to

Quiraing

negotiate, but keep to the inner edge and it is done. From now on the narrow path, hugging the side of the cliff, makes for an exhilarating walk. Beside the path grows the pretty rose-coloured alpine campion.

Wild strawberry

The path comes to the bottom of The Prison, a huge mass of rocks that looks like a fortress. The narrow path into its confines is eroded in places. It is fairly easy to ascend, but the trip down is not for the faint-hearted. Any worries can be overcome by scrambling down on your behind.

On the other side of the main path, opposite The Prison, stands The Needle, a huge pillar of rock the sides of which seem inaccessible to all but the ravens. More than two dozen of these birds glide around the cliffs and their guttural grunts echo eerily back from the sheer rock faces. Below The Needle lies a steep slope of scree and grass; by ascending this and then passing behind The Needle you can reach The Table. This is a large, oval-shaped, bright green table of grass surrounded by towers and pinnacles of rock and castellated crags. It was used in times past for hiding hundreds of cattle from raiders – and in modern times for a game of shinty.

Do not despair if you find the scree slope too daunting for The Table can be seen again later on the walk. Continue along the path. Climb a short scree slope, then walk along another narrow path with steepish slopes dropping away to the right. Climb a fence and walk on along a muddy part of the path to an unexpected wall. Beyond lies a quiet, high-level grassy valley with vertical rock faces to the left and huge heather-clad rocky outcrops to the right. Here, where you are sheltered from the wind, the sun is exceedingly warm. Follow the path as it climbs out of the tiny glen until you reach the lower slopes of Meall na Suiramach. Sit and enjoy the extensive views over the Minch to the Isle of Harris and Lewis.

Turn left and begin the long, long climb up the grassy slopes to the summit of Suiramach. The path comes close to the cliff edge and from here you can see several lovely dark blue lochans that were hidden from sight as you walked through the valley, now far below. A cairn crowns the summit. From the edge of the cliff you have an excellent and exciting view down to The Table, oval-shaped, bright green and grassy. It is surrounded by towers, pinnacles and castellated crags. Look for the sturdy rose-root growing in the many crevices on the rock faces of a wide ravine that runs down to The Table.

From the summit you strike down and inland over the moor, well away from the continuing cliff edge. There is no obvious path but aim for a sheep-track on the rocks ahead, remaining on the same contour. Walk on till clear of the cliffs and you will see the car park far below. When in line with the vehicles, begin to descend the heathery slopes that you memorised at the start of the walk.

This is a stimulating four-mile walk, one not to be missed. Walking boots and a good waterproof are needed.

4 miles
3 hours

4. Walk through Quiraing, starting from the northern end of the Range

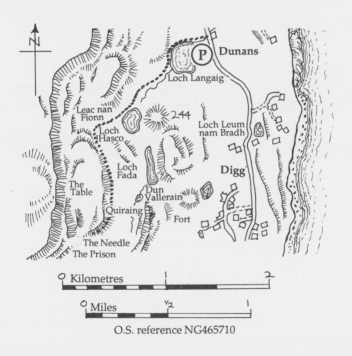

O.S. reference NG465710

Drive along the A855 northwards from Staffin. You pass the primary school on the right and then a lochan on the left. Once past this pretty sheet of water, park in the large lay-by on the left-hand side of the single-track road. Walk on until you come to a cart-track leading into the hills. From here you have a wonderful view of The Table, in Quiraing. With this mountain stronghold ahead you can be sure you are walking in the right direction.

Turn left along the track. In August it is banked by heather, shading from white to deep purple. Young meadow pipits and twites flit about it. Walk along the track and continue when it becomes a path – sometimes a muddy one – passing the large wind-tossed Loch Langaig. Where the ground is very muddy after a wet day, move up into the heather, using any narrow path that keeps in the same direction as the more obvious one.

Heather

Follow the path as it makes a wide swing round a very wet depression and then continue as it begins to climb through the heather above the secluded Loch Hasco (the loch of the high place). A down-draught from the steep slopes purls the water in this lovely mountain pool. Sometimes a sudden storm comes hurrying through a gap between the steep slopes. The wind pushes a curtain of rain along and tosses it like a flimsy veil in all directions.

The path comes to a fence stretching from the skirts of Sròn Vourlinn (the mill point or promontory) to a foot or so into Loch Hasco. Beyond, the path passes through tall colourful heather to the grassy slopes above. Follow one of several paths which lead through a deep grassy hollow where rabbits scramble across the springy turf. Climb out the other side and walk along the path as it swings round, contouring another deep hollow littered with boulders. Keep to the highest path so that you do not lose height.

Proceed along the path as it swings to the left and into the valley immediately below the great buttresses, pinnacles and crags that crowd around The

Meadow pipit

Table. These rough-faced towering guardians of The Table have tiny patches of grass, bright green in the sun. Now the mist comes down from Meall na Suiramach. It trails between the pinnacles and hangs over The Table. Ravens fly in and out of the low cloud, their raucous grunts echoing back from the craggy surfaces. One flies down and picks at a carcass at the bottom of the slopes.

Join the path that runs throughout the mountain range, past The Needle and the steep scree climb that some take to reach The Table. The path continues past The Prison and you can walk along the narrow path for as far as you wish. You will, after a mile, come to the road that crosses the pass between Staffin and Uig – or of course you can return the same way and regain the lay-by where you have left the car, avoiding a tedious walk along the road.

The return walk from the Staffin Road to The Prison is just over three miles and takes about three hours depending on how many pauses you take.

3 miles
3 hours

5. Walk to Loch Hunish from the Phone Box near Duntulm

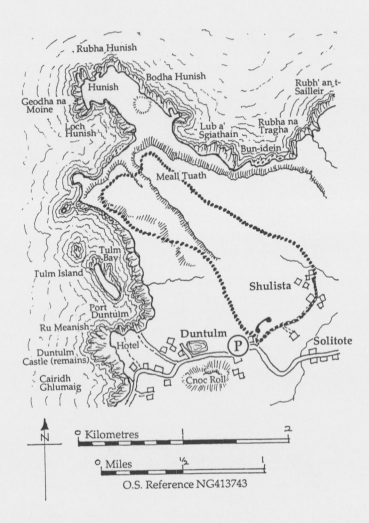

Rubha Hunish

Bodha Hunish

Rubh' an t-Sailleir

Hunish

Geodha na Moine

Loch Hunish

Lub a' Sgiathain

Rubha na Tragha

Bun-idein

Meall Tuath

Tulm Bay

Tulm Island

Shulista

Port Duntulm

Ru Meanish

Duntulm

P

Solitote

Hotel

Duntulm Castle (remains)

Cairidh Ghlumaig

Cnoc Roll

N

Kilometres   1   2

Miles   ½   1

O.S. Reference NG413743

Rubha Hunish (Bear's or Hunn's Point) is the most northerly point on Skye. Loch Hunish lies south of the point and can be reached by walking across the moorland north of Duntulm. Park on the verge by the phone box, which has a tin-roofed shed behind it. A narrow single-track road, well-signposted, leaves the A855 here. Walk along the heather-bordered road to its end by Willie MacLeod's croft house. Ask permission to walk past his byre and he will take you, most courteously, across to his gate and point out another that gives access to the open moor.

Walk up onto the heather slopes and follow a good sheep-track that passes through banks and banks of heather where the air is full of the noise of bees. The tiny path leads to a fence across the headland, with an immense drop into the sea. Look for the layering of the strata on the cliff face – below the headland turf it lies aslant and half-way down the cliff the columns drop vertically into the sea.

Turn left and follow the fence along the cliff tops. Out to sea lie vicious jagged rocks with a warning bell astride the largest. Gleaming white gannets, with black-tipped wings, fly high above the water and then dive into the wave-topped Minch. An eagle flies overhead, its feathers brilliantly gold in the bright sunlight. The little path, easy to walk, passes through more heather and then comes to a lovely sun-filled grassy ravine just made for picnics.

Gannet

Walk on and look down on the grassy spit of land, Rubha Voreven, that projects out into the blue-black sea as a storm cloud races above. Continue along the little path, beside the fence,

23

until you reach the disused coast-guard hut which looks out over the sea to Harris and the many islands between. After a long look at the glorious extensive views over the water, take the old path (used by the coast-guards some years back) for your return to the car.

This is where the hard walking begins. Walk a few yards until you see the Duntulm Castle Hotel and continue in that direction along the indistinct path for as long as you can discern it. Then look to the left of the hotel for the tin-roofed shed with the phone box beside it where you left your car – one-and-a-half miles across the moor. Keeping in line with the shed, walk across the heather, bog myrtle and asphodel of the moorland. It is occasionally wet and frequently hard walking. Cross the fence and keep to the higher ground on the left, well above the damp flat valley. A gate beyond the shed leads to the lay-by and your vehicle.

Bog asphodel

This is a good walk of four to five miles with spectacular views for all the way. On a day of sunshine and showers you will see many rainbows – some bowed, some high in the clouds and others flat and seen just above the waves. Attempt the walk only if you are happy finding your own way, using very sketchy paths or none at all, and if you have a good sense of direction.

4¹/₂ miles
5 hours

6. Walk to Duntulm Castle (the castle on the round hillock)

Ru Meanish

Duntulm Castle (remains)

Hotel

P

Cairidh Ghlumaig

Lub Score

Bealach Iochdarach

Cemy

Museum

Monument to Flora Macdonald

Peingown

Clachan

Kilometres

Miles

O.S. Reference NG410740

Duntulm Castle

Park in the large lay-by on the A855 just beyond the road sign for Duntulm Castle (if travelling in the direction of Staffin from Uig). There is also space to leave a vehicle on the verge a few yards along the road. Pass through the clearly marked wooden entrance gate perched high on the cliffs and walk up the path towards the dramatic ruin. Herring gulls and black-backed gulls glide below you, hardly making progress against the strong south-westerly wind. Milk thistles, buttercups and clover flower among the cliff-top grass. Across the wind-tossed sea lie the Ascrib Islands, with the Waternish peninsula beyond. A flock of starlings fly down to the black rocks and quickly rise again. A kestrel, intent on seeking prey, flies into the midst of the flock and the smaller birds whirl and twist as one. The kestrel, unperturbed by the confusion it has caused, continues hunting.

Walk through a kissing-gate and on past the cairn which commemorates the MacArthurs, who were pipers to the castle. The castle lies ahead of you. One large wall and several smaller pieces of masonry still stand, all that is left of the lofty buildings that were once the proud stronghold of the Macdonalds, Lords of the Isles. Shadowed by the isolated walls is an arch with a window in it. Look down the small flight of stone steps which lead to a vaulted chamber. Beyond the ruin the cliffs drop sheer into the sea – in great turmoil today. What tales the remaining stones could tell. If you get to the castle early, before any other visitors arrive and disturb the eerie atmosphere, you feel that at any moment an 18th-century piper or perhaps an armourer might appear from behind the ruined fort.

To return, take the path to your left that runs beside the fence and has a rope rail to the seaward side. This leads to a little beach and a small harbour, Port Duntulm. The sand is black and so are the boulders and about these fly, excitedly, many young rock pipits. Sit here and watch the fulmars on Tulm Island taking off from their ledges on the tall cliffs. They fly like small gliders, making good use of the winds, and then return to their ledges. Far below them on more black rocks sit shags, black silhouettes against a brilliant blue sea. Out in the Minch an oil tanker negotiates its way between the many rocks and islands and far beyond lies the grey outline of the Outer Hebrides.

On the other side of the beach, a flock of herring gulls sit facing into the wind. A large number of oystercatchers feed and pipe, and overhead fly a pair of curlews, calling as they go. A buzzard soars above them all, its feathers turning fawn in the bright sunlight. Follow the cart-track which leads from the beach past a reed bed where a reed warbler clings with one leg bent grasping a stem, chattering continuously. It disappears from sight but not from sound. At the end of the track, a gate leads you to a driveway at the side of the hotel, where pied wagtails flit ahead and whinchats sit on the wire fence. On reaching the road, turn right and walk back to your car.

Buttercups and clover

27

From here you might like to drive the one-and-three-quarter miles to Kilmuir Cemetery where Flora Macdonald is buried. An inscription below the Celtic granite cross reads, 'She is a woman of middle stature, soft features, gentle manners and elegant presence'.

The half-mile walk to see Duntulm Castle is not to be missed but do not forget your waterproofs.

Seagulls

¹/₂ mile
1 hour

7. Walk to Beinn Edra (the hill between others) from Uig via Glen Conon

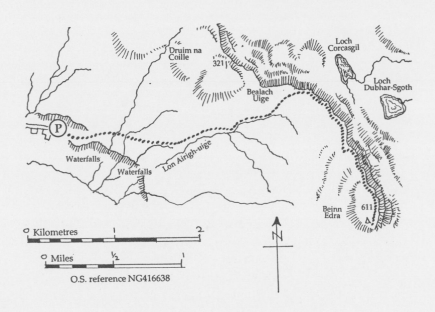

Kilometres
Miles
O.S. reference NG416638

Drive northwards along the A856 towards Uig. Cross the bridge over the River Conon and turn right, ascending the single-track road that hairpins for much of its first half-mile. Drive on through Glen Conon to the gate at the end of the road. Open the gate and drive through onto a cart-track and leave your car in the large reinforced lay-by. Far over the moorland lies the summit of Beinn Edra, the mountain that lies between Quiraing and The Storr, and which is the goal of this walk.

Hoodies

Walk on along the cart-track. Goldfinches feed on the seeded thistle heads, pied wagtails chase flies over the damp turf and house martins dart overhead. Beyond the next gate, a pair of hoodies probe the sod and a seagull careens across the sky. Walk on to the next gate, beyond which a brown peat-stained burn races over its stony bed on its way to join the River Conon. If it is in spate, find the most convenient crossing place so that you arrive at the other side dry-shod. The noise of a chuckling burn accompanies you for much of the way.

The track now swings out into the open moorland where heather, tormentil and eyebright grow, with lousewort flourishing in the wetter areas. After a mile, the track dies out as it comes to the edge of some extensive peat cuttings. Keep well above these as you walk to the wire fence ahead.

Cross the fence and walk beside it down to the edge of the Lon Airigh-uige, another tributary of the Conon. (Count the fence-posts so that you can find again the indistinct end of the track if the mist should come down.)

Follow the narrow, faint path that keeps close to the gurgling stream for most of its length. It is easy to walk and passes through banks of heather. The path comes close to the foundations of some old crofts.

Lady's mantle and eyebright

It enters a hollow where the burn descends in a series of pretty cascades, the sparkling water tumbling through gardens of ferns, heather, golden saxifrage, alpine lady's mantle and long-stemmed daisies. In spring, primroses carpet the ground. On the lip of a fall, a dipper sits sifting the surging water for food. Its plump round body, with white bib and chestnut belly, bobs up and down when it pauses from its hunting. Its mate flies from above and hurries a short way downstream, disappearing into a hole in the bank where an overhang of heather hides it from dangerous intruders.

Alpine lady's mantle

Above the falls you have a first dramatic sighting of the jagged tops of Quiraing and of the northerly Macleod's Table. Continue along the tiny track, keeping to the left side of the stream. Here in the moss grow dog lichens, milkwort and butterwort too. The little stream becomes narrower and in many places underground with the path continuing above – out of sight but not out of sound. Bilberry, heavy with fruit, now covers the moorland. Continue climbing until you reach the apparent source of the stream and then ascend the steepish slope ahead. From the top you can see Uig Bay and the Ascrib Islands, with the Waternish headland beyond. In the other direction lies Staffin Bay and the mainland mountains over the sea. To see both shores of a peninsula at once is always a delight.

Overhead glide a pair of buzzards, crossing the glen without flapping their wings. Walk straight uphill (no path now) through both types of club-moss and more alpine lady's mantle until you reach the ridge. Walk to the cliff edge and with care look down on the flatter land around Staffin, with its many lochans reflecting the blue of the sky. Look across to the great vertical cliffs of Quiraing, with their grassy tops sloping steeply to the precipitous edge.

To the right along the ridge lies the summit of Beinn Edra, less than four-fifths of a mile, with its wonderful views in all directions. Overhead, several young ravens dive acrobatically, twisting and turning as they delight in the air currents, occasionally giving the guttural grunts so evocative of mountain fastnesses.

It can be a little unexciting to return from a walk by the same route but here it is the only way you can avoid a long hard trek on the road. The journey back has great compensations, with lovely views of Uig Bay and its sheltering cliffs ahead of you all the way.

This is an enjoyable six-mile walk, taking four hours, along an infrequently used path that takes you deep into the silence and solitude of the moorland, with increasingly exciting views as you climb. Waterproofs and good walking boots are sensible wear.

As you drive south, back along the A856, make a short diversion to see the standing stone, Clach Ard. This is reached by turning right along the B8036 and then taking a right turn signposted Tote. The stone stands half a mile along the road. Look for the intricately carved symbols on its face.

6 miles
4 hours

8. Walk to Beinn Edra from Balnaknock

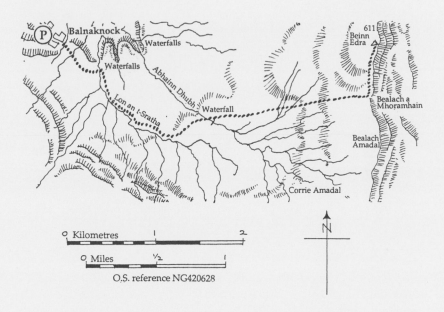

Kilometres

Miles

O.S. reference NG420628

Leave the A856 at the turning signposted Sheader, south of the River Conon above Uig harbour. Balnaknock is two-and-a-half miles along the single-track road, which passes through charming hollows where ancient hazel trees grow in profusion. Park in the lay-by just before the last house and walk on along the metalled road for 20 yards or so. Pass through a gate on the right that gives access to a wide grassy cart-track. A wren flies fast and direct, with tiny wings whirring, across a small stream.

33

Look across Glen Conon to three magnificent waterfalls, swollen with overnight rain, raging tempestuously down the lowest cliffs of Ben Gorm. Close by, a pair of mistle thrushes, when disturbed, fly from the path to a willow tree thriving in a narrow gully beside the track.

Pass through the next gate and walk on until the track is bisected by the hurrying Lon an t-Sratha. Cross this by well-placed large stones, some of which may be under water if the burn is in spate.

Dippers

Walk on along the cart-track and pass through the next gate. The path continues beside the racing burn where a pair of dippers hunt for insects, running into the fast-flowing water and then curtseying, spasmodically, on top of a spray-splashed rock. The cart-track runs for nearly a mile before it peters out.

Continue walking in the same direction, making full use of heathery hummocks to get you across the moorland, circumventing peat hags and boggy areas until you reach the waterfalls on Abhainn Dhubh. These lovely sparkling falls of water tumble in great elegance, and with dancing joy, through heather. Spend some time in this sun-trap savouring nature's perfection. Perhaps you will see the pair of dainty grey wagtails that haunt the rocks in the middle of the turbulent hill stream. They dart upwards to catch flies and return to the boulders unconcerned by the water splashing over their feet.

If the burn is not in spate, cross below the lowest waterfall and climb up the bright green turf dyke that strides uphill to some low cliffs. The dyke continues beyond the crags to the final slopes of Beinn Edra. If you cannot cross the river because it is surging too strongly, walk upstream for a quarter of a mile until you can wade the burn or cross on boulders.

Then strike across to the left over heather and crowberry moorland – very wet in places – until you reach the dyke. The crowberry is laden with black edible berries, beloved by the red grouse, but today there is no sign of the birds. Only their droppings tell us they have been here.

The dyke stretches away uphill until the Bealach a Mhoramhain (the pass of the big river) is reached. From here walk to the left, over club-mosses, alpine lady's mantle and bleached grass, until you come to the cairn on Beinn Edra

Waterfall on Abhainn Dhubh

(2,006 feet). From here there are magnificent views of Uig Bay and the sea beyond, and of fearsome cliffs stretching away to the north and south. Walk to the cliff edge – with great care, and if the wind from the west is not too strong – and enjoy the glorious views below and out across to Rona, and to Gairloch and the Torridons on the mainland.

Return by the same route.

This is a splendid seven-mile walk taking four to five hours. Do it in August when the heather moor is a blaze of purple and pink.

7 miles
4^1/$_2$ hours

Walks 9 and 10

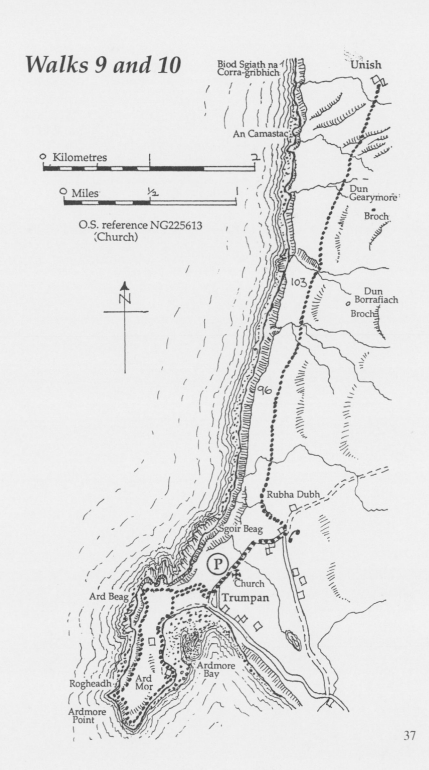

Biod Sgiath na
Corra-gribhich

Unish

An Camastac

Kilometres

Miles

O.S. reference NG225613
(Church)

N

Dun
Gearymore

Broch

103

Dun
Borrafiach

Broch

96

Rubha Dubh

Sgoir Beag

P

Church

Trumpan

Ard Beag

Ardmore
Bay

Rogheadh

Ard
Mor

Ardmore
Point

9. Walk from Trumpan Church to Unish, Waternish

Park in the large lay-by opposite Trumpan Church on the most westerly point of the single-track road that runs along the west coast of the Waternish peninsula. Sit in the car and watch the stoat that lives in the wall. It runs along the top of the stones, a long furry pencil with two stand-up ears, a smart, white chest and a long tail with a black tip. It uses the latter as a rudder as it moves among the boulders.

Stoat

Walk up the long, narrow and very straight road northwards. In the pastures to the right grow potatoes and oats and among the latter flourish many corn marigolds. The lane is bordered with tansy and meadow sweet and below these tall plants thrives the large-headed, exotic zig-zag clover. Swallows race overhead feeding on the plenteous midges but many more gather on the telephone cables. Curlews call from over the moor and birds fly low heading for the seashore. A small flock of shags, keeping close together with long necks stretched out, head for their colony on the rocks around the bays of Ardmore Point.

Where the road turns sharply to the right, take a left turn through a gate onto a good cart-track. Follow this as it leads out into extensive heather moorland, now a magnificent purple. Pass through the next gate and walk on to where the bubbling calls of curlews come from deeper into the moor. Enjoy the views across the sea to the Outer Hebrides.

Look for the memorial, beehive-shaped, on a hill to the left of the track. Climb the wire fence where the barbs have been covered and follow the little track up to the top. The plaque commemorates Roderick MacLeod of Unish 'who fell in the second battle of Waternish which was fought on this moor against the Macdonalds of Trotternish about 1530'. The cairn was erected by American clansmen. As the sea fret drifts in, one can almost hear the battle cries.

Walk on along the track, passing a ruined croft, close to a wide, shallow burn. Stonechats give their alarm call, which sounds like a pebble striking a rock. Higher up, and away from the path, stand the bare remains of Dùn Borrafiach, a broch which gave magnificent views to its defenders of approaching marauders. Close by the path, beyond the broch, look for the neat stacks of peat drying.

Continue along the easy-to-walk track until you see another broch, Dùn Gearymore, to your right. This is more accessible. Little remains of the original edifice, but the rabbits and whinchats do not seem to mind. Among the litter of boulders grow a variety of ferns and foxgloves in flower. The site is a splendid viewpoint for the moorland around and the extensive seascape. Could the broch ever have been taken by surprise?

From now on you can enjoy several good views of the lighthouse on Waternish Point, with its white walls and green door. The path turns towards the east and comes to the ruinous settlement of Unish. The foundations of

Foxglove

several crofts huddle together close to another pretty stream and over to the left stands a large and rather imposing ruin. All is still and deserted and rather sad. As dense sea mist comes in, blotting out the lighthouse and the ruins, even the wheatears, meadow pipits and curlews are quiet.

This is an easy walk of six miles, with good views, that takes you back into Skye's past.

Wheatears

6 miles
3 hours

10. Trumpan Church and Walk to Ardmore Point

Trumpan Church lies on the western coast of Waternish. Drive along the B886 and continue on the single-track road signposted Ardmore and Trumpan. Park in the large space opposite the church ruins. Walk round this windy graveyard with its magnificent view over sea and moorland. Read the inscriptions on the sturdy tombstones, some of which sit athwart the wind and the rain as if, even after death, the robust folk of Skye defy the elements.

Trumpan Church

A gable end and a few crumbling walls, one with a pretty window opening, is all that is left of the church. One sabbath day in 1578, so the history books tell, a party of Macdonalds from Uist in the Outer Hebrides landed in the bay and surprised the local MacLeods at worship. They set fire to the church, burning it and all but one of the congregation within. A woman escaped and raised the alarm, and all the raiders were killed. They could not get away because their boats were beached.

The stones are heavily encrusted with the lichens *Usnea* and *Xanthoria*, and grass grows along the top of the walls. Overhead, curlews fly and their haunting calls travel over the quiet scene. Pied wagtails run across the turf after insects and rabbits play just outside the graveyard; nature does not seem influenced by the sadness of the place.

Walk back down the steep hill, where in spring primroses and violets flower, and take a cart-track on the right. Ten feet along this, look for a gap in the wall on the right and climb over a semblance of a stile to a distinct path that runs away to the right. In a field below, a small herd of Highland cows and their bull graze. They look ferocious but are quite uninterested in the walker. Follow the path as it drops quite steeply to a wire fence. Walk beside it, event-

Highland cattle

ually crossing it and continuing along the path that now follows the curve of a small bay. The beach is made up of large round black boulders and masses of brown seaweed. Here, on black outcrops of rock that jut into the sea, sit a colony of shags together with herring gulls, all facing the same direction. A grey seal swims around, peering at us as we pass.

Follow the path as it climbs Ard Beag, keeping within the unobtrusive wire fence beyond which the cliffs drop away to rocks and sea far below. The path is bordered with a glorious array of summer flowers, the purples of self-heal, scabious, clover and heather contrasting delightfully with ragwort, hayrattle and eyebright. Look for the pretty felwort; both purple and white grow here. To the north, towards Waternish Point, huge waterfalls tumble down the cliffs. Water from one is caught by the wind, which funnels the spray into the air. Out to sea a pair of gannets dive for fish and far beyond lie Uist and Harris.

Continue along the path and look for the natural arch at the bottom of the cliffs ahead. Shags sit on the arch to dry their wings. Then they fly low across the water, their wings hitting the sea with resounding claps as they go.

The little path descends to another bay of black rocks and then climbs above the natural arch before continuing to Ardmore Point. The walker has excellent views of the small

Natural arch towards Ardmore Point

islands of Clett, Mingay and Isay and the cliffs below Beinn Bhreac on the west side of Loch Bay. Follow the little path as it keeps just above the shore of Ardmore Bay. Walk past the once elegant house, which belonged to the laird and overlooked the bay. Beyond, the path becomes a track and passes a small harbour for the house, then skirts a ruined building that was the steading of the larger house.

Stand here and enjoy the activity on the shore. Curlews, oystercatchers, herons, herring gulls and hoodies feed. A black-backed gull flies into the air, dropping a shelled creature onto a rock. As it smashes, the gull gobbles up the contents. A sandpiper calls hauntingly from its reach of the beach. A small flock of dunlins rise from feeding in the tidal gutters and fly as one round the bay, just above the waves. They manoeuvre skilfully until they land and then, because of their colouring, are lost to view.

Pass through the gate and walk across the pasture straight ahead, picking up the path used earlier at the foot of Ard Beag. Peep into the bay to see if the grey seal is still swimming, competing with the shags for fish.

This is a glorious two-and-a-half mile walk, with wonderful views over the sea and the islands – best done on a sunny day.

2¹/₂ miles
1¹/₂ hours

11. Walk from Waternish House Gate to Loch Losait

Driving north on the Waternish peninsula, turn right at the T-junction immediately after Lusta. A quarter of a mile further on, park neatly in a large passing-place close to an exit gate from Waternish House. Enjoy the wild raspberries growing along the roadside, then walk along the road and over the bridge, and look upstream through rhododendrons and larch to the pretty waterfall. Leave the road and take the cart-track to the north of the burn and pass through the gate that gives access to the open moor. In August the heather is a wonderful sight, shading from white

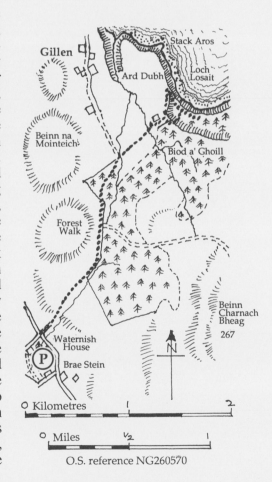

O.S. reference NG260570

45

Wild raspberry

through pink to pale mauve and deep purple. The lower slopes support many sheep. Overhead a buzzard ignores the attentions of two hoodies and several black-backed gulls. Look back to the bay with its little islands off Dunvegan Head. From this vantage point they show their steep cliff faces.

Pass through the next gate and continue along the pleasing track now bordered by Forestry Commission conifers on the right. To the left, the wide verge is a colourful garden of ragwort, heather, hayrattle, kidney vetch, scabious and sneezewort yarrow interspersed with lush ferns. Meadow pipits twitter on the moor and then fly over the track and settle on a branch of a spruce. Later, conifers border the track on both sides. A pair of bullfinches call and fly from the trees to sit atop the heather. They stay so long that we are able to see their lovely colouring.

After a mile of walking, suddenly and surprisingly quickly, you see a new stretch of the sea that surrounds this lovely island – ahead and to the east is Loch Snizort and the Ascrib Islands, their grassy-topped cliffs seemingly very

Kidney vetch, sneezewort, hayrattle, ragwort

46

close in the rain-washed air. The track begins to drop downhill as the trees to the left cease. Look for the little beck that feeds a deep pool. Here on its banks grow masses of felwort, the bright blue gentian.

Now the path passes through moorland again and the marching rows of conifers are far over to the right. On the fence close to the track a pair of stonechats sit, still accompanied by several youngsters. The track divides, the left-hand one going to Gillen. Take the track to the right. This is not reinforced but is easy to walk along. In wet places, cross on timber suitably placed. Several burns bisect the path but they take only a stride to cross. Along the path silverweed grows. On the left are traces of old crofts.

The now grassy track runs along the top of cliffs giving delightful views into Loch Losait. Huge banks of heather overhang the way, with hazel and willow on the shore side. The track makes a dog-leg turn before dropping steeply to the shore, and here another pair of bullfinches flit from bush to fence calling their soft, clear 'wheep, wheep'. The deeply water-rutted track now passes under hazel and birch with

Bullfinches

wood sage growing below. As you descend, the calls of curlews, gulls and oystercatchers greet you from the black sandy beach.

What a glorious bay this is. Behind the beach is a wide grassy sward. This is backed by many rows of immature conifers that are the haunt of goldcrests, willow warblers and whinchats. Above are steep slopes covered with willow, birch, rowan and oak. Higher still rear the castellated and pinnacled tops of Beinn an Sguirr. Out to sea gannets soar and dive and a seal's head emerges for a short time. Rock pipits chase each other over the huge black boulders that litter the shore. This glorious secluded bay is the place to picnic, day-dream, sunbathe and perhaps swim.

On your return, walk back along the shore and take the raised track at the side of the last row of conifers. This gradually ascends until you are looking down on the tops of the trees. The track veers slightly to the left and then turns steeply and sharply to the right. It climbs through bracken to a small wet area, which is easy to cross. After scrambling up a short slope, you reach the cart-track once more.

This is an excellent four-and-a-half mile walk that takes you right across the peninsula, leads you through both coniferous and deciduous woodland and brings you to a hidden bay that you might have to yourself all day.

4¹/₂ miles
4 hours

Walks 12 and 13

Groban na Sgeire

Lampay

An Dorneil

Lovaig Bay

Souterrain (remains)

P

Claigan

Rubha na Gairbhe

Beinn Mhic Uilleim

Rubh' an Goirtein

Loch Corlarach

Loch Suardal

Dun Fiadhairt Broch

An Dubh-aird

The Cottage

Gairbh Eilein

Dunvegan Castle

Jetty

N

Kilometres

Miles

O.S. reference NG490276
(Jetty)

12. Walk to the Coral Beach, near Claigan, north of Dunvegan

Much of Skye's coastline is composed of magnificent cliffs. There are bays and inlets where the shore is boulder-strewn, with some black sand. But it is quite different at the Coral Beach.

Drive past Dunvegan Castle car park on the A850 and continue along the narrow single-track road that runs along the east coast bordering Loch Dunvegan. Great banks of heather edge the road and extend over the moorland as far as the eye can see. The road crosses Loch Suardal (green sward-dale), where a heron rises from the water and flies up the burn. It continues past Loch Corlarach to the remote hamlet of Claigan. Where it turns sharp right a cart-track leads off left towards the shore. There are two large signs here, one advertising Claigan Nurseries and the other indicating 'Coral Bay'. Park at the side of the cart-track

Heron

so that you do not obstruct access, or tuck in neatly to the grassy verges beyond the bend in the road. The ground is hard here and half a dozen or more cars can make use of it.

Walk down the cart-track past hawthorns laden with berries. Young goldfinches flit through the branches, their favourite diet well supplied by the wealth of hardheads, thistles and ragwort that grow along the verges of the track. Pass through the kissing-gate and walk along the wide and somewhat stony track. Cross the small beck by well-placed stones and look upstream to see the brilliant display of touch-me-nots. Curlews call from the pastures on either side and then a pair of the brown, bulky-bodied birds fly low overhead, calling as they go.

Pass through the next gate. Down to the left, cattle graze on the turf just above the seaweed-covered pebbly shore. Heather and low-growing willow cover the sides of the track, which is now grassy and pleasing to walk along. Gorse bushes thrive on either side. A stoat runs fast across the track and is immediately lost in the undergrowth. Ahead lies the first expanse of coral beach, a pale yellow colour lightening the greyness of a cloudy day. Go onto the beach and pick up a handful of the 'sand'. It is hard to touch and

Coral

composed of minute particles, all different in shape. It is calcified seaweed; scattered among the myriad of tiny white shapes are small shells and little polished pebbles. Herring gulls fly overhead and a wheatear flits from one clump of seaweed to another after small molluscs. Rock pipits fly low about the black boulders.

Cross the pasture to the right to a wall behind a ruined croft. Walk up a narrow path beside the wall until you reach a gap. Pass through and follow the little path that runs above the shore through heather and then continues across springy turf beside the sea. A grey seal noses out of the water as if curious to see what the walker is about.

Follow the path as it rises a little and then ahead lies a glorious curved bay of 'coral' – pale gold and inviting – overlooked by a craggy hill. Where the tide comes over the 'coral', the water turns to turquoise. Another seal, or perhaps the same curious one seen earlier, rises half out of the water at our approach. Climb the hill and enjoy the splendid view over the wedge-shaped islands of Isay, Mingay and Clett with Ardmore Point beyond. Look down to the racing water between the coral beach and the grassy-topped islands named Lampay. Beyond them towers Dunvegan Head and in the distance the Outer Hebrides are a smudge of grey.

Walk on down the side of the hill, where primroses bloom in spring, and on to the end of the peninsula. Here in the crevices of the black crags grow the pink and white stonecrop, sea pinks and sea campion. A tern flies low over the choppy sea uttering its harsh, short cry.

Tern

This glorious walk can be enjoyed by young and old. It is easy walking all the way, but take your waterproofs and perhaps a beach mat on which to sunbathe – the coral is very hard! The best beach is almost at the headland, so make sure you walk far enough.

4 miles
3 hours

13. Dunvegan Castle, the Grounds and the Seals

A visit to Dunvegan Castle is a good choice when the day dawns with sea mist blotting out the landscape. The castle, well-signposted, lies on a rock half a mile north-west of the settlement of the same name. It has ample parking, with a gift shop and a rest-aurant. The castle is open for most of the summer, except Sundays, between 10 a.m. and 5.30 p.m.

Dunvegan Castle

The approach to the castle is along a drive lined with rhododendrons and a yellow potentilla. Once inside, a sturdy oak staircase, with the MacLeod motto 'Hold fast' above a bull's head at the top, takes you to the upper floors, through which you can wander at your own pace. Note, as you move around, the narrow stone circular steps that lead invitingly to the upper rooms of the Fairy Tower. From the window beyond the staircase see the pretty burn cascading in a mass of white foam. The next room, the dining room, has some magnificent ancestral portraits and a massive oak sideboard.

In the drawing room you will find displayed the Fairy Flag, considered the most treasured possession of the clan. It is treasured because it is supposed to have special powers to protect the MacLeods. And so named because it is said to have been given to a chief in the 14th century by a fairy. Close by, more stone stairs in the thick wall ascend to the keep. Close by, too, is the dungeon, 13 feet deep. Prisoners were dropped through a trap in the guardhouse floor, the only access, and left to die of cold or starvation.

In the North Room look for the spectacular embroidery of the family coat-of-arms done in wool by the daughters of the 24th chief. Enjoy the lovely view of Dunvegan Loch from this room.

In the passageway beyond is a display of St Kilda relics, St Kilda, a group of islands 40 miles out in the Atlantic, belonged to the MacLeods for at least four centuries. From the passage you can get onto the Gun Terrace and see the freshwater well, the vital requirement of any fortified building. From this terrace you can see the sea gate, only entrance to the castle until 1748, when the landward entrance was built.

To visit the seal colony after leaving the castle, follow the directions for the jetty. On your way, look back for an excellent view of the remains of the massive curtain wall that once totally enclosed the rock on which the castle was built.

Seals

A small outboard motor-boat takes you through Loch Dunvegan to the seal colony. Here, when the tide is low, huge rocks and islands emerge covered with dense seaweed. Dozens of common seals and greys lie in the sun, stretch, scratch and cavort playfully. Baby seals struggle up the slippery sides onto the upper 'deck' to join others. The boatman takes you close and then steadies the boat so that you can photograph them.

On your return to the jetty, follow woodland paths to the north of the estate. These traverse the side of the loch, where Highland cattle graze and from where you can see the seals again. Hooded crows and oystercatchers feed on the shore and along the side of the track there are wild raspberries to quench your thirst. The track joins a single-track road that runs along the side of the loch.

Walk back along the track and take a small path that leads into the rhododendrons and then comes to a splendid viewpoint overlooking the castle. Before you leave the peaceful grounds, stroll to the other side of the castle to enjoy the formal round garden beneath the cascading waterfall, the haunt of a grey wagtail. Above the garden stands a massive ancient beech. What a story of the MacLeods it could tell.

14. Walk to the Lighthouse at Neist Point opposite Waterstein Head

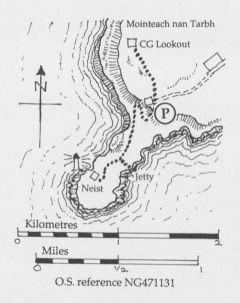

O.S. reference NG471131

Travel south from Dunvegan and leave the A863 close to Lonmore and drive along the B884 through Colbost and Glendale. Continue along the single-track road, taking a left turn signposted Neist Point. This narrow metalled road runs high above Loch Mor and then drops downhill, passing through the settlement of Waterstein. The car park lies at the end of the road and overlooks the spectacular 971 feet of Waterstein Head across Camas nan Sìdheah.

Walk out of the far end of the car park along a concrete path and follow it where it turns left before descending steeply, by means of steps and a slope. Look to the left to see the huge hoist used to winch goods for the lighthouse down from the top of the cliff to the flatter ground below. The path clings to the cliff and here ferns and heather fill the crevices.

The narrow path crosses a wide grassy plateau, where sheep graze, then ascends to hug the edge of a tall hill. Beyond this the path slopes downhill, crosses a wide grassy area where the lighthouse keepers play golf and wheatears and meadow pipits dally. It then leads to the lighthouse, which is of major importance to the shipping using the Minch. The living quarters, smartly painted in cream and orange, cosily huddle around the tall lighthouse of the same colour. Between 2 p.m. and an hour before sunset you can join a tour of the lighthouse.

Neist Point Lighthouse

From the lighthouse, walk on over the turf to see the extensive views out to sea. Notice the huge horn, which sits atop a concrete building, used when there is fog. Return to the lighthouse and walk along the reinforced path to the jetty. From here you can see Waterstein Head 'front-on'. Gannets dive into the deep dark waters below, which so accurately repeat the colour of the stormy sky. Look further along the cliffs to the peat-stained waterfall cascading into the sea.

After enjoying the vista, walk back along the path that skirts the hill. Then take a distinct sheep-track to the left and continue to the edge of the cliff. Look to the small headland

across the seething water where cliffs, like huge organ pipes, descend vertically. A bright orange lichen grows high up, looking like a wide shaft of sunlight shining on the cliff. Fulmars sit close to the rock face on a narrow ledge. Many more fly around on stiff glider-like wings, sailing and planing with great agility. Look for the colony of shags sitting on the rocks at the foot of the cliffs, with more flying in to join the crowd already there.

You obtain a good view of the lighthouse from the cliffs above the car park, which you reach by a narrow path. The path leads out onto the grassy headland above the cliffs seen earlier from Neist Point. Among the moorland grass grows the bear berry laden with bright red round fruit.

This is a good walk for spectacular views of the cliff-girt most westerly point of Skye. For once walking boots are not needed but do not forget your waterproofs because some of Skye's worst gales occur here.

1^1/$_2$ miles
1 hour

15. Walk from Ramasaig to Lorgill River

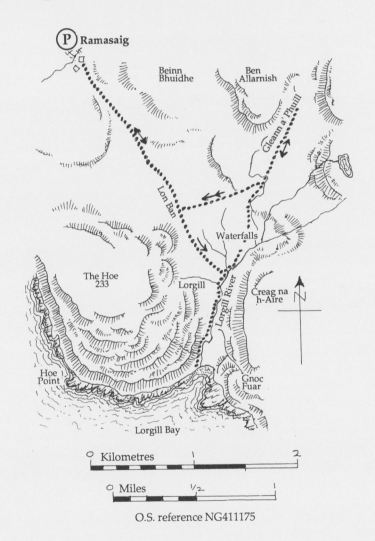

P Ramasaig

Beinn Bhuidhe

Ben Allarnish

Gleann a Phuill

Lon Ban

Waterfalls

The Hoe 233

Lorgill

Lorgill River

Creag na h-Aire

N

Hoe Point

Gnoc Fuar

Lorgill Bay

Kilometres 0 1 2

Miles 0 1/2 1

O.S. reference NG411175

Ramasaig lies at the end of a very narrow single-track road. Leave the A863 at Lonmore and drive along the B884, taking a left turn signposted Borrodale one mile beyond Glendale. The tiny moorland road comes close to Loch Eishort. A female hen harrier pauses, with wings faintly quivering, as she hovers over the heather. She quarters the slopes, pausing expectantly, and then glides off, showing the perfect symmetry of her long dark wings and thin tail.

Park just before the gate across the road where there is a large lay-by, but do so neatly so that you do not obstruct vehicles passing on their way to the farm buildings. Walk through the gate and continue along the unmade road, by-passing the farm buildings and continuing straight ahead to a gate in the fence. The wide track keeps just below the rocky slopes of Beinn Bhuidhe. (Do not follow the tractor marks that lead towards Ramasaig Bay and then suddenly cease.)

The track, called Lòn Bàn, is a pleasure to walk along as it passes through the heather moorland. After a quarter of a mile look back for a glorious view of Neist Point lighthouse on its bright green finger of grass, almost encircled by a deep blue sea. Close by you can see the sheer cliffs of Waterstein Head and its smooth grassy top. Further along the track, look across to the left to Macleod's Tables. The track, about a mile-and-a-half long, begins to drop downhill, coming to a deserted croft house beside the River Lorgill. If you intend to walk along the cliffs towards Macleod's Maidens try to cross here, but you may have difficulty if the burn is in flood because it is then wide and fast.

If you cannot manage the crossing, then continue walking downstream following the indistinct path over the springy turf that borders the meandering river. You walk into the sun; ahead lies Lorgill Bay cradled by huge cliffs, and all is perfect. A raft of eiders floats on the sparkling sea. Wheatears and rock pipits flit about the black boulders of the shore. Shags fly across the sea just above the waves and the piping of oystercatchers fills the air. Red rattle grows in the wet flushes by the river. This marvellous sun-trap is the place to picnic.

Return along the river bank to the deserted croft house and then walk upstream into Gleann a' Phuill, following good sheep-tracks that lead through heather and bracken. From the track near the river bank you can view six magnificent waterfalls. They fill the ravine with a great noise and their waters are deeply stained with peat. In the wall of the ravine above the top waterfall grow rose-root, large headed devil's bit scabious and various ferns. Walk on uphill through bracken and stand on a small hillock covered with heather, willow and bear berry. From here you can see four more foaming waterfalls. Below the hillock grows a gracious aspen. Continue walking uphill beside the tempestuous burn, climbing through secluded ravines where racing water passes through a necklace of deep pools and rocky falls.

When you can leave this delightful seclusion, strike west over the lowest outcrops of Ben Allarnish to reach a turf bank that crosses the heather and brings you to the track, Lòn Bàn, at the point where it started its descent to the croft house.

This is a glorious walk for sea views, surging rivers and fine waterfalls. As always in Skye, walking boots and waterproofs are advisable. The walk is five miles in length, and can take all day when the sun shines.

Large headed devil's bit scabious

5 miles

16. Walk to Healabhal Mhor (Macleod's Table North 1,538 feet)

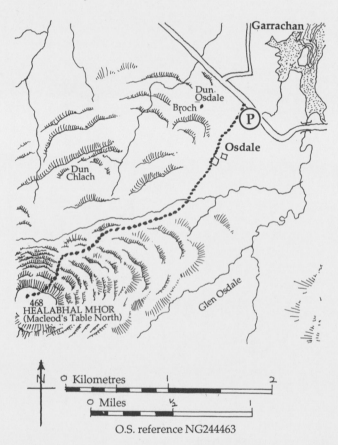

O.S. reference NG244463

Drive along the A863 and turn left at Lonmore. Follow the B884 as it comes close to an inlet of Loch Dunvegan. From here both of Macleod's Tables can be seen. Pass the new water treatment building and park in a large lay-by a quarter of a mile along the road. Walk on to a gate that gives access to a cart-track that leads towards two ruined buildings – all that is left of the settlement of Osdale. Here a short-eared owl flies close to the vegetation, moving silently, quartering the heather for voles. Nine young red grouse scurry between the clumps of vegetation. They are seen one moment and then lost to sight.

The track soon deteriorates into a sketchy path overrun by rabbits – including a black one. From the lonely, deserted buildings, look back to the loch and the scattered houses around its shore. Beyond the croft, walk towards a gateway (no gate) in the fence and follow the track down to the burn, a tributary of the Osdale River. A buzzard rises, soars on the thermals and then sets off in the direction of Glen Osdale.

Cross the pretty burn on stones. If the gaps are too wide, place extra boulders in the shallow water. Rowans, willows and birch clothe the steep sides of the ravine and huge overhangs of heather crowd the top edge. Follow the sheep-tracks that lead from the water and continue across the heather moorland; the bog myrtle is covered with catkins, and among the yellowing bent grow purple milkwort and pale lilac eyebright. Make your way diagonally to the right, across the moor, keeping an eye on your destination, the top of the Table. As you ascend, try to memorise your route to help you when you return because there are no paths on this walk.

The walk across the moor, though wet in places, presents no difficulties. You come to the bottom of a fairly sharp heather-clad slope. Here look for white heather, with bright green leaves, growing among the pink flowers. Grouse droppings lie in little clearings beside the clumps of heather but there is no sign of the birds. Find the

Bog myrtle

63

easiest way up the slope and then climb the rougher but less steep ground above. From here the views are splendid. Dunvegan Castle lies on the other side of its loch. To the left you can see the 'seal islands' and further along the shore the coral beach, a pale lemon in the morning sunshine. Beyond lie the islands off Waternish, with Ardmore Point and Waternish Point in the distance. Out to sea the hills of the distant Hebrides are strung along the horizon.

Continue climbing upwards, finding the best way round the rocky outcrops and ridges of rock, keeping an eye on the summit for as long as it is visible. Pause regularly as you climb and look down on the lovely Loch Bracadale, with its many islands floating on silver, tranquil waters. And look to the far left, where the jagged tops of the Cuillin Hills for once are free of cloud.

Then the steep climb to the Table lies ahead. Keep well to the left away from the edge of the cliffs that drop sheer. Suddenly the flat top lies at your feet. Stroll across the mossy plateau to the far side, keeping to the left of a small lochan. Look for club-mosses growing among the moss. From here you can see the grassy top of Waterstein Head away to the

Macleod's Tables

right. To the left lies Healabhal Bheag (Macleod's Table South 1,601 feet), a mountain with steep sides and jagged slopes. It has a smaller table but is 63 feet higher than the one you are standing on. Beyond the tops of these two giants the sea sparkles in the sunshine. Far to the left lie the mountains on Rhum. Overhead a pair of peregrines glide and then swoop dramatically after prey and are lost to sight over the edge of the summit.

Return across the Table and look for the ruined crofts far below. When you have your bearings, begin your descent.

This is a splendid four-mile walk that takes as many hours if you can find a sheltered rock for a picnic. The views are spectacular and the walking not too strenuous for most of the way. Walking boots and waterproofs are a must.

4 miles
4 hours

Walk 17

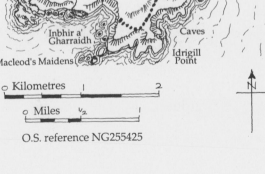

Loch
Bharcasaig

Caves

Abhainn Bharcasaig

Cave

Cnoc na
Pairce

Geodha na
h-Aibhne

Waterfall

Forse Burn

Beinn na
Moine

Beinn na
Boineid
371

Brandarsaig
Bay

Ben
Idrigill

Cave

Natural
arches

Caves

Camas na
h-Uamha

Ard
Beag

Waterfalls

Caves

Inbhir a'
Gharraidh

Idrigill
Point

Macleod's Maidens

o Kilometres 1 2

o Miles ½ 1

N

O.S. reference NG255425

66

17. Walk to Macleod's Maidens from Loch Bharcasaig

Drive along the A863 north towards Dunvegan. From this road there are dramatic views; in the distance, across Loch Bracadale, lie Macleod's Maidens, striking pillars of rock beyond Idrigill Point and the object of the walk. Turn left at Roskhill, following the signpost directions for Roag. Look for a thatched barn on the left. Turn left

Thatched barn

again at Orbost and continue along a narrow bumpy cart-track behind Orbost House towards Loch Bharcasaig. Leave the car on the left on a wide flat area of turf, which is quite firm for parking.

Walk on down the track towards the bay, where the waves come in gently on the black sand and pebbles and where common seals peer curiously at activity on the beach. A pair of oystercatchers call noisily from the turf on the edge of the cliff and the sea smells fresh. Follow the path as it begins to climb, with rows of coniferous trees to the right and splendid views across the little bay to the left. A family of tiny goldcrests search, meticulously, each twig of larch for insects, whispering quietly as they go.

The track moves into the forest and the sea views are gone but ahead Beinn na Boineid rears into the blue sky. Wrens call from the undergrowth beside the path. As the way begins to climb, you catch brief glimpses of the sea. The track drops again before leading out of the forest and at last there are clear views of the sea once more. Walk to the edge of a pretty burn, then cross it by convenient boulders. Beyond is a kissing-gate to the open moor.

Follow the narrow track that climbs the slopes ahead. It is well-cairned and leads you along the driest way. On either side the moorland is gashed with dykes – some as yet unplanted by the Forestry Commission.

In a few years, when the trees are fully grown, the views will be lost and with them the tormentil, milkwort, bog asphodel, orchis, eyebright, dwarf willow and heather. But it is slightly reassuring to look back from here at the mature forest, where the foresters have made a great effort to provide a pleasing variety of green foliage and plantation shapes. In time the scars on the hillside will go and hopefully viewpoints will be created as the forest grows.

Thyme, hard fern, beautiful St John's wort and heather cover the slopes traversed by the narrow but distinct path. Angry meadow pipits scold as we come too close to their brood, hidden safely below the vegetation. Pass more ditches and planting. Then a gate leads onto moorland slopes and the gashes are no more.

Pause or picnic at the sheepfold high above Brandarsaig Bay and look across the brilliant blue water of Loch Bracadale to Harlosh Point, Harlosh Island and Tarner Island. High over the cliffs of the bay a pair of buzzards soar on the thermals and keen as they fly.

The excellent path continues downhill to two narrow burns. Cross these on boulders and climb to a large area of springy turf where rabbits sunbathe and banks of heather cover the rocky slopes. Continue along the path, enjoying views across to Wiay Island and Oronsay, with its cliff and rock formations shaped liked a fortress.

Then follow the path as it climbs behind Ard Beag through a short but delightful heather glen where grow primrose and violet leaves. Look for the pretty falls which tumble through heather-banked small ravines. Ahead is the first glimpse of the open sea – and the force of the wind confirms what our eyes tell us. To the left lie the cliffs of Idrigill Point.

From now on there are no more cairns but the track leads over the turf into the wind and then out onto a grassy plateau. With great care look over the edge and down to the three Maidens far below. Great white-topped breakers crash around the pinnacles. A huge wave disturbs a shag sitting on a smaller rock and it flies to the top of one of the three Maidens.

Macleod's Maidens

69

Kittiwakes nest on grassy ledges high up on one rock stack, well out of reach of summer spray. Look north to where a long streaming waterfall tumbles over the cliff edge, much of its water being funnelled by the wind high into the air. Move to the heather-covered slope just north of the promontory. Here, out of the gusting wind, you can enjoy a good view of the spectacular rock formations and also of another waterfall, its water, too, being syphoned upwards.

The walk from Orbost to the Maidens and back is ten miles and takes five hours. Choose a sunny day for best views of the sea and its islands and a day that is not too windy if you wish to get near enough to the cliff edge to enjoy the fantastic rocks. The route is easy to find and easy to walk, with just a little extra agility required to cross the burns if they are in spate.

10 miles
5 hours

18. Walk to Ullinish Point and Oronsay

Leave the A863 at the turn signposted Ullinish just beyond Struan. Drive along the single-track road for a mile and park behind the Ullinish Lodge Hotel. Walk along the track that passes between two outbuildings and when it comes, very shortly, to the gate of a house turn sharp, almost acute, left and follow a narrow grassy track that leads to a small gate which gives access to a very narrow road. Turn right and follow the road for 100 yards until it ends at a house. Pass through the gate beyond the house and follow the cart-track across pasture land. Skylarks, disturbed, rise into the air singing sweetly. Walk on to the next gate.

O.S. reference NG325377

71

Beyond lies a rough track that gradually ascends the grassy cliff, where innumerable deep mauve scabious flower. To the left is a good view of Ardtreck Point lighthouse and the entrance to Loch Harport, where gannets dive. In the far distance the jagged tops of the Cuillin can be seen in their entirety, no cloud obscuring their magnificence. Keep to the path which, wet in places, hugs the cliff edge. Ahead lies Oronsay, an island that can be reached at low tide. It is wedge-shaped, with a gentle grassy slope rising up on the landward side and vertical cliffs to seaward. To the west lies the island of Wiay, with Idrigill Point distant in the haze of a summer's day. To the far left stand the formidable cliffs below Fiskavaig.

If the tide is out, pass through the little gate and cross over to the island. With care climb up the grassy slope and enjoy the glorious view of sea and sky.

This is a short stroll, best attempted when the tide is out and very pleasant in the evening. It is a mile each way, taking an hour.

2 miles
1 hour

19. Dùn Beag Broch, Bracadale

A broch was a defensive tower, dating from the Iron Age. Dùn Beag (little fort) broch stands high on its hill, with much of its stonework intact, inspiring your imagination with thoughts of times long gone. It stands proudly overlooking Loch Bracadale, where fleeting sunshine picks out the blues and greens of islands and dramatic headlands.

Look for the ancient monument sign on the A863 just north of the hamlet of Bracadale. There is excellent parking, a picnic table and a good view both out to sea and towards the broch. Cross the road and pass through the kissing-gate. Beyond, a wide, dry, grassy path leads through heather and bracken to the foot of the dun.

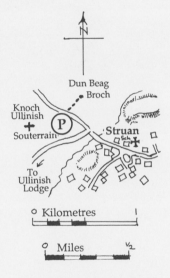

O.S. reference NG338387

Dùn Beag was built by farmers and herdsmen, perhaps between 400 BC and 200 BC. From then on, at various times and at least until the late Middle Ages, it was used as a refuge against attack or in times of danger. It would have housed a small community who farmed the surrounding area. The massive drystone circular wall is some 13 feet thick. The long narrow entrance passage was the only external opening into

73

the wall and could be easily defended. Inside and to the right of the passage is a well-preserved chamber or 'guard cell'. To the left of the entrance, built within the thickness of the wall, are the remains of the stone staircase, which would have given access to the top of the wall and perhaps the upper floors.

The broch was excavated between 1914 and 1920 and many treasures were found including iron

Dùn Beag broch

spears, knives for hunting and fighting, crucible and ingot moulds for bronze working, an antler pick for digging, a stone lamp, coins and some personal ornaments made of stone, bone, bronze, gold and glass.

Stand on the wall and look out to sea to Ardtreck Point and the cliffs below Fiskavaig to the south-west, to Macleod's Tables to the north-west and to Idrigill Point due west. Inland over Beinn nan Braclaich a pair of buzzards soar and sail, harried by ravens, the deep calls of the latter and the eerie cry of the buzzards sounding the same today as they did to iron age man.

$^1/_2$ *mile*
$^1/_2$ *hour*

20. Fernilea, Portnalong, Talisker Bay, Carbost, Fernilea

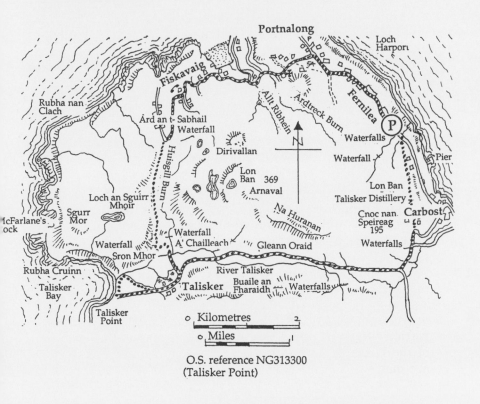

O.S. reference NG313300
(Talisker Point)

Fernilea, a small skein of houses, spreads out along the narrow road that runs beside Loch Harport, on its south-west side. Park in the large lay-by, where soil and rock have been removed, on the left-hand side of the road, six-tenths of a mile beyond the top of the steep hill out of Carbost. As you walk on along the road towards Portnalong, enjoy the profusion of summer flowers that bedecks the roadside banks and verges. You will see early purple orchis and spotted orchis, hemlock, touch-me-nots, beautiful St John's wort, tansy, foxgloves, hardheads, dog daisies, hayrattle and sneezewort. Stretching away from the roadside into the meadows and pastures on either side is meadow sweet, the most abundant of flowers, still newly-flowered and filling the air with a sweet aroma.

Follow the narrow road as it moves out onto moorland, where bog asphodel and cotton grass grow in the wetter areas. Look for the neat conical stacks of peats and for wild valerian, ragged robin and bog myrtle. Look, too, for the haycocks close to the croft houses, where the land is better drained.

Purple orchis

Turn left by the shop at Portnalong (harbour of ships) and walk past the red-roofed, grey-walled school and past the church. From the top of the next slope the island of Oronsay comes into view, and Macleod's Maidens, the large pinnacles of rock beyond Idrigill Point, over Loch Bracadale. From the bottom of the hill you can see Fiskavaig Bay. Continue along the single-track road, enjoying the ever-extending views over the loch. Here grow dog roses, clover and hawkweed, and creamy-coloured honeysuckle clambers over willow.

The hazels, willows and birches along the roadside harbour great tits, blue tits and blackbirds. On the wires leading to the croft houses sit linnets and numerous young meadow pipits and chaffinches.

At the tip of the hairpin bend beyond Fiskavaig, walk straight on along a cart-track that leads out onto the open moorland, with Beinn Bheag to the left. Here, in contrast to the luxuriance of the roadside, fewer wild flowers thrive. Look for male fern growing in the banks of the track, with the barren fronds prostrate on the ground and the fertile ones springing up from the same clump. Look, too, for heath and heather, now both in flower, and the pretty tormentil growing among the purple flowers. On the open moor, meadow pipits and wheatears abound. Look for stonechats and whinchats sitting atop heather shoots. Cotton grass flourishes in the many wet areas and red rattle in the ditches beside the track.

Where the track ends, a narrow path continues over the moor and drops steadily down Huisgill, giving splendid views of waterfalls tumbling down the steep slopes on the other side of Talisker. Follow the springy turf path as it descends in a wide zig-zag, coming close to the lovely waterfall on the Huisgill Burn, which races through heather-clad slopes. At the bottom of this fall is a sun-filled grassy hollow – just the place for a picnic before continuing into Talisker.

Turn right at the end of the track just beyond the white gates of Talisker House and walk along the track in the direction of the beach. Above, to the left, is the huge mass of Preshal More. About its tops soars an eagle, unworried by the harrying of a pair of ravens. Follow the track as it passes Talisker House and then take a path that leads off to the right signposted 'the scenic route' to the shore. This delightful path at first takes you through bracken and then continues along a causeway beside the fast-flowing, deeply-stained Sleadale Burn. A twite sits on a thistle head and then leans over to obtain the seeds. The banks support a wonderful variety of wild flowers that please the eye with their brilliance of colour and profusion. Vast reed beds stretch away on either side and play host to reed buntings and sedge warblers.

As the path moves through the reeds, the sea is still unseen but is not unheard. Cross the footbridge and climb a stile, following the little track to the beach in Talisker Bay. To the north, an elegant waterfall tumbles vertically down the steep cliff face. To the south are the tortured rocks of Talisker Point. Between lies a black sandy shore. Out across the blue waters of the bay lies mountainous South Uist.

Walk across the beach to the cart-track that takes you back to Talisker House and then continue straight ahead along the narrow road through Gleann Oraid. The road climbs and climbs past more spectacular waterfalls. Behind lie the blue waters of the bay and towering away to the right are the slopes of Preshal More. Overhead a pair of peregrines fly with fast-beating wings. Then the birds glide forward, rolling slightly from side to side, sporting together and joining in acrobatic gambols. Suddenly they stop and 'stoop' in a great downward rush on a meadow pipit. Fortunately for the pipit, they fail to catch it. Very soon a third bird – perhaps a youngster –joins them and they continue their aerial frolicking.

Peregrine falcon

Continue climbing the narrow road where meadow pipits and wheatears flit and a pair of hoodie crows wing across the rough moorland grass. Then the road begins to descend, passing the right turn to Glen Eynort. To the right lie the Cuillin Hills, their tops veiled in soft cloud. Walk on towards Carbost and, where the road swings sharply to the right, bear off left along a cart-track that ends at a house. Walk along the path behind the house and then continue along a raised dyke that swings along the lower slopes of Cnoc nan Speireag. This very pleasant high-level walk gives good views of Carbost below and the waters of Loch Harport. Follow the path along the dyke for nearly a mile and then, as it comes near to the road, follow a narrow indistinct path leading down to a red metal gate onto the road. Walk on for 100 yards to where the car is parked.

This splendid ten-mile walk (taking five to six hours) is full of contrasts. It could be done as two shorter walks, Portnalong to Talisker Bay and Carbost to Talisker Bay, on each walk returning the same way.

Bullfinch

10 miles
5¹/₂ hours

Walk 21

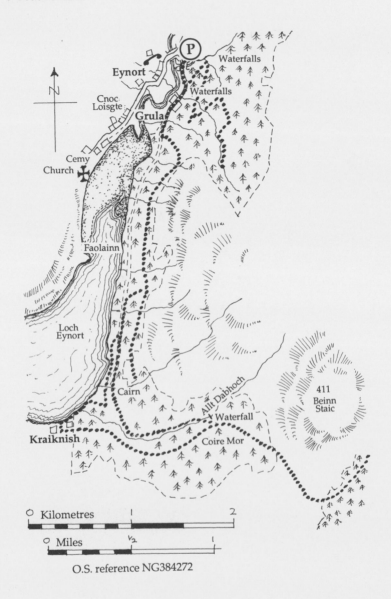

Waterfalls

Eynort

Cnoc Loisgte

Grula

Waterfalls

Cemy
Church

Faolainn

Loch
Eynort

Cairn

Allt Dabhoch

411
Beinn
Staic

Waterfall

Kraiknish

Coire Mor

Kilometres

Miles

O.S. reference NG384272

21. Walk through Forestry Commission Woods by Loch Eynort

When a gale blows and the wind gusts up to 50 miles an hour – as it occasionally does in Skye – the walker is advised to find a sheltered walk. A walk through Eynort forest is an ideal choice, the trees breaking the force of the wind and giving some protection from the worst of the rain.

The O.S. Map for South Skye (one-and-a-quarter inches to the mile) shows a good circular walk through the forest. It does not exist in fact. The harvesting of trees obliterates tracks for some time and you should be prepared for some of the tracks and rides to cease suddenly. The views you can enjoy also change with time. Some are lost as young plantations grow upwards, but new ones are created as mature trees are removed. Nevertheless all the tracks are pleasing and you should attempt as many as you can.

To reach the forest, drive to Carbost and then follow the road signs for Eynort. A single-track road traverses Glen Eynort, with the Eynort River, swollen and angry, racing over its bed far below to the right. Where the road divides, take the left-hand fork and park in a largish space beside the racing water of a feeder stream hurrying to join the Eynort.

Walk on along the road and take the first left-hand turn, which climbs up the hillside in a steep hairpin. Here the trees have been cleared and the resulting extra light has encouraged a profusion of flowers to cover the slopes. Fireweed and foxgloves contrast pleasingly with ragwort. Heather grows in great tufts, even thriving on the stools of felled trees. Beech trees, used as nurses for the earlier crop, now appear spindly and lacking in foliage as they are blown violently by the fearsome wind.

A flock of young goldfinches chatter in a silver birch and then launch themselves, still twittering, into the forceful wind. Long foaming streams slash the slopes and race beneath the forest road. A bridge carries the walker over the magnificent waterfall on the Allt Dàidh. A kestrel flies ahead, perhaps hunting for the many short-tailed voles living in the dense moss that covers the way where the tarmac ceases. To the right of the road, the steep slopes drop down to the village of Eynort, the houses lining the shore road tucked snugly under Biód Mór.

Kestrel

The road ends at the edge of a deep cleft and beyond it a steep crag rears abruptly upwards. Here the kestrel, seen earlier, has its brood.

Return to the bottom of the steep hairpin taken at the start of the walk and continue ahead on the forest road, pausing at the foot of the spectacular fall on the Allt Dàidh. The roaring water, tumbling vertically, is stained with peat. Walk on through several buildings and take the left-hand turn to enjoy a second short walk with splendid views. Follow the track as it climbs higher and higher, looking down on the loch and on Faolainn, a green finger of land projecting into its waters. Here again the low-growing plants flourish luxuriantly where the hillside has been harvested. This track ends at a tumbling burn in a small ravine and the walker must return to the forest road once more or clamber down the steepish slope to the section of the road seen below.

This lower road passes deep into mature conifers and you no longer enjoy the bright colours of the wild flowers. Goldcrests and coal tits si-si-si conspiratorially from the branches just overhead, while a buzzard circles high above, filling the forest with its eerie keening. Where the forest road divides, take the upper path and continue through the trees. This road climbs and climbs and reaches another large cleared area of the forest. Sit here on a convenient log and look down on Loch Eynort where it makes a dog-leg turn towards the open sea – a delightful view.

Walk on along the road as it climbs higher, past the waterfall on Allt Dabhoch where the foaming water descends wide steps of rock and contrasts charmingly with the dark green foliage all about. Overhead a pair of peregrines tumble in the wind, dark arcs against the greyish sky. In half a mile the forest ends. Walk on for 200 yards along the track beneath Beinn Staic to see Glen Brittle far below and beyond it the white-topped waves at Mussel Scalp. To the left lie the Cuillin Hills, austerely veiled in low cloud.

Return along the forest road to the waterfall. Here a track goes off to the left and descends steadily through another area of cleared forest. Once more a myriad of multi-coloured flowers bedecks the forest floor. Ahead, magnificent views of Loch Eynort can be seen for the whole length of the track. Here a sea eagle sits on a tree stump enjoying the end of the rain. Close to, the bird seems enormous. It sits quite still, only occasionally stirring on its bright yellow feet and turning its head so that we can fully appreciate its cruel beak. Eventually it takes off, rather heavily at first, and then soars out over the loch. This lovely track ends at a farm gate with no sign of the connecting path (shown on the O.S. Map) to the forest road that returns to Eynort.

Here a decision has to be made, whether to return to the waterfall a mile or so back up the long sloping track or to climb over the gate and walk down the steepish slope to the beach. If you choose the latter, you will have to scramble or paddle across the Allt Dabhoch where it races across the pebbles to the sea. After crossing the burn, strike up for 20 yards through the jungle of vegetation to join a good track, the lowest of the forest rides, which strides into the forest and joins the main road through the conifers.

These walks through Eynort forest total eight-and-a-half miles.

Goldcrest

$8^{1/2}$ *miles*
$4^{1/2}$ *hours*

Walk 22

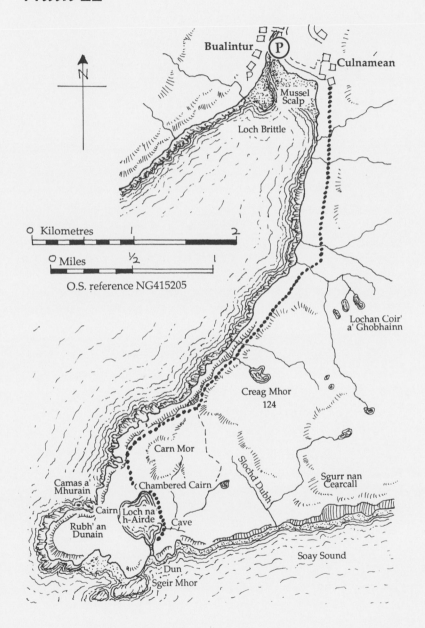

N

Bualintur

Culnamean

Mussel Scalp

Loch Brittle

Kilometres

Miles

O.S. reference NG415205

Lochan Coir' a' Ghobhainn

Creag Mhor
124

Carn Mor

Stochd Dubh

Chambered Cairn

Sgurr nan Cearcall

Camas a' Mhurain

Cairn Loch na h-Airde

Cave

Rubh' an Dunain

Soay Sound

Dun

Sgeir Mhor

22. Walk from Glen Brittle to Loch na h-Airde

The single-track road to Glen Brittle leaves the B8009 at the village of Merkadale, which lies south-west of Carbost. Pause at this junction and look down the placid Loch Harport to Macleod's Tables away to the north-west. The road swings over the moor, which is covered with yellowing grass. Then it drops down and down through Glen Brittle Forest, where the sunlight catches the tips of the trees. The conifers, in spite of their regularity of planting, size and species, soften the bleak valley sides.

After ten miles, the road swings in a curve and comes close to the River Brittle. A rainbow arches over the road. Park in the large lay-by at the start of the beach and walk on along the track ahead. Below lies the wide sandy beach where the waves come rolling in slowly and where the swimming is safe.

Continue through the camp-site and climb the stile behind the public toilets. Turn right and follow a path that keeps Loch Brittle in sight for all its length. After rain the track is very wet and it can be walked comfortably and safely in wellington boots. These enable you to cross, dry-shod, the numerous streams and burns that race pell-mell down the moorland slopes to the sea. One or two of these make spectacular descents over the cliffs and can be seen from the path. Do not attempt to wade the Allt na Buaile Duibhe but walk upstream to a wooden bridge, hidden from the path at one point by banks of heather.

Over the bog myrtle, now heavy with yellow catkins, flit numerous dark meadow brown butterflies. A kestrel flies up out of the vegetation and over the bay, its feathers tinged with orange as they catch the sunlight. Follow the path as it climbs steadily upwards – the slopes to the right dropping down to steep cliffs. These are wonderful gardens of heather, ferns, orchis, yellow vetch, bog myrtle and willow. Far below on rocks uncovered by the receding tide greater black-backed gulls sit and preen.

Immediately after crossing a racing stream the path divides, the left fork making its way inland past a small lochan. This is an attractive walk but those who follow it lose the magnificent views over Canna and Rhum, both of which stand out startlingly clear after the last shower has washed the air. The lower path continues above the cliffs. By a drystone wall the path divides again, the lower one taking a rather breathtaking course close to the edge of the precipitous cliffs and the other over the tops, and safer. If the track is dry and your nerve is good, the cliff-edge walk gives excellent views of a dozen or more shags sitting far below with their wings held out to dry. Look at the delicate spleenwort ferns growing in the crevices of the overhang of Carn Mór. Here bluebells, primroses and violets grow in the spring.

Walk on along the path (the upper and lower soon join) as it continues along the cliff-tops, skirting immensely sheer, narrow chasms that stretch yawningly down to the quiet sea. On the narrow ledges and crevices of the chasms grow rose-root and sea campion, and on the grassy tops the pretty felwort flowers. The path continues above the side of a small bay where a massive flat rock, washed by the sea, seems made for sunbathing and where a pair of divers swim, occasionally raising themselves high in the water, flapping their wings and pointing their bills upwards. Here in the sheltered corners of the cliffs thrive more rose-root and English stonecrop.

Stonecrop

87

Follow the path until it comes to a drystone wall, beyond which, to the right, is the path to the bay. To the left lies Loch na h-Airde, where a heron stands in shallows beyond the great reed that is colonising the nearer edge. Do not pass through the gap in the wall but walk up a short path to the left that leads to a mound of stones. This is a magnificent chambered cairn, with standing stones for an entrance and a passageway on the other side. In the centre, now roofless, grow a rich variety of ferns.

From the top of the cairn there is a wonderful view to the nearby islands and to the Outer Hebrides. A petrel flies silently overhead. It is so quiet here that you can hear the fishermen speaking to each other in the boat just outside Loch Brittle.

This excellent six-and-a-half mile return walk follows distinct paths, but not quite in the direction shown on the O.S. Map. It is ideal for a day when the clouds are on the Cuillin but the sea is bathed in sunshine.

6^1/$_2$ miles
3 hours

Walks 23 and 24

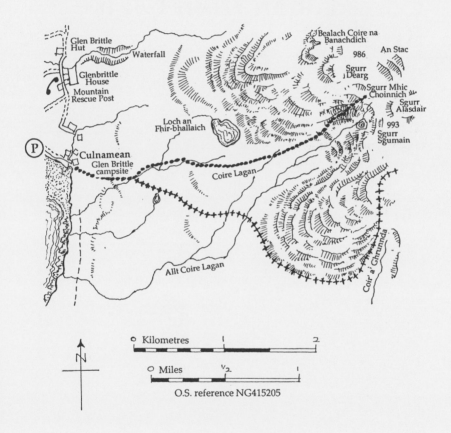

O.S. reference NG415205

23. Walk to the Loch in Coire Làgan from Glen Brittle

Walk through the camp-site at Glen Brittle, after parking in the lay-by just outside. Climb the stile behind the toilet block and walk straight ahead up the steep, eroded track. Take the left branch when the track forks and continue on to a little stream, crossing it by rocks. From here, for quite half a mile, work has been done to improve the surface of the track and small drainage channels have been cut and lined with stone to take off some of the excess water.

Walk on for half a mile along the gradually deteriorating, rocky path passing Loch an Fhir-bhallaich away to the left. From here the path begins to climb more steeply but the sight of the rim of the corrie challenges you and encourages you to keep on. Cotton grass and bog asphodel grow extensively on either side of the way, reminding you how very wet the terrain is. Meadow pipits flit from plant to plant and fill the air with their sweet calls.

Cotton grass

Few cairns line the way but the path is easy to follow and the white-topped water falling down the smooth massive slabs of rock keep the walker climbing in the right direction. To the right, on the other side of the Làgan Burn, is the climber's rocky path to the cliffs of Sron na Ciche.

Bog asphodel

When you scramble to the brow that has been encouraging you forward, you find there is another beyond. The way continues over scree and small boulders, then comes close to the tumbling burn. You reach the next brow, then realise there is still another to surmount. But, as before, the track leads up and over and finally the lovely turquoise-blue lochan lies in a sheltered basin to the right.

This is a great reward for a longish trek, uphill all the way. As the sun comes out and the mist lifts, the water marvellously reflects peaks, pinnacles and soft white cotton-wool clouds in a deep blue sky. Look back out over the rim of the corrie to an equally blue sea and to the Outer Hebrides delicately and invitingly stretched out along the horizon. To the north-east corner of the corrie lies the rock shoot where several intrepid climbers ascend. They move over the rock scree, slowly, like brightly coloured spiders, always edging upwards. Then they cross over the shoot, carefully, bearing to the right and are lost to sight as they continue on to Sgurr Alasdair – the highest peak in the Cuillin Hills. Regularly a climber returns down the long run of scree, taking less than half the time to ascend.

It is exciting to watch these agile folk. Some walkers may be tempted to climb too, but for those who prefer to enjoy the game from the touchline the mountain vegetation is all around to be enjoyed too. Alpine lady's mantle, rose-root and a low-growing bramble thrive in the crevices between the boulders. Juniper spreads over rocks, and heather and thyme flourish in the sheltered environment. Look for the rare rock whitlow grass, now bearing delicate white flowers.

Mist drifts in between the pinnacles and obscures the climbers and the tops and then drifts away, leaving the sun to shine down into this lovely, secluded hollow. High overhead – even higher than the tops – six ravens fly, their croaking calls echoing around the corrie.

This is a straightforward, pleasant climb along a rough path demanding walking boots. Take waterproofs, but if the weather deteriorates come back. It is a four-mile round walk and takes four hours if you allow time for enjoying the treasures of perhaps the most attractive of the Cuillin corries.

4 miles
4 hours

24. Walk to Loch Coir a' Ghrunnda from Glen Brittle

Park in the large lay-by before the camp-site at Glen Brittle. Walk past a lovely hay meadow full of summer flowers and various species of grass and on through the caravans and tents, before crossing the stile behind the public toilets. Walk straight up the steep moorland slope, following the eroded track to where it divides. Here continue to the right. After 20 yards the track dips down to a stream easily crossed on rocks. Walk on along the track, passing a small blue lochan on the right where a red-throated diver stays close to its youngster. Continue along the track for four-fifths of a mile. After a wet night this can become very muddy but a sunny morning and a drying wind soon improve its condition. At Allt Coire Làgan you cross the turbulent burn by numerous well-placed rocks.

Follow the track beyond and aim for a seemingly precariously balanced rock seen clearly on the horizon. Just before this boulder is reached, look for an indistinct path to the left. This becomes a clear pathway in a few steps and steadily begins to climb, joining a path coming from the left. Proceed along this track for nearly a mile, pausing frequently to enjoy the magnificent views seawards. Soay lies below with its many coves, bays and harbour. Much of the island is covered with heather moorland spangled with small lochans, which sparkle in the brilliant sunlight, and there are areas of deciduous woodland. The Outer Hebrides can be seen clearly across the open sea and looking southwards you can view the many peaks of the Grampians.

Golden eagle

When you first see the entrance to Coir a' Ghrunnda, follow a path that climbs steeply to the left, hugging the sheer rock face of the skirts of Sgurr Sgumain. This is a beautiful path, passing through heather, hard fern, tormentil, foxgloves, eyebright and devil's bit scabious. Look for the spleenwort fern growing in the dark recesses below the overhanging rock. Do not follow the cairned path that continues ahead because the way up the slopes from here can present difficulties. Overhead glides a golden eagle – a very large black silhouette against the blue sky. It flaps its great wings just once and sails across the heavens before being joined by another. After more soaring, they both glide off towards the mainland.

For half a mile the path climbs steeply and then passes through some very rough scree, but from this high-level way there are exciting glimpses down into the moon landscape of the corrie. The huge high-sided rock amphitheatre seems almost unreal but if you are to ascend to the loch above you will find just how hard and real it is. Sgurr nan Eag is the guardian of the other side of the spectacular corrie and every now and again its top loses its veil of mist revealing its steep, rocky slopes.

Once over the scree the tiny path, generally visible but not invariably so, crosses a massive rock field. At the far side, the path moves upwards through great patches of alpine lady's mantle, bilberry laden with purple fruit, stone bramble, alpine rock cress, wild thyme and common wild thyme. Keeping to the left of the streaming burn, which tumbles in great white plumes down the sheer slopes, look for a narrow gully, which will enable you to ascend the final vertical rock face. Once up this moderately easy scramble, follow the tiny path as it weaves through boulders where procumbent juniper hugs the rocks and rose-root grows. After some more easy scrambling the path leads to the edge of the lovely remote Loch Coir a' Ghrunnda. This is an extraordinary hollow surrounded by the towering and castellated sides of Sgurr Alasdair. The mist flows over the water and suddenly blots out the jagged tops above and then just as quickly moves away and the basin becomes sun-filled once more.

This is a wonderful corner deep in the hills to observe nature at her most wild and wilful but if the mist continues to funnel into the hollow it is best to begin the descent and return to enjoy the extensive seascape.

This seven-mile return walk takes as many hours if you are going to enjoy the views and the wonderful mountain vegetation. It is a hard walk with a loch in a magnificent setting as the ultimate reward.

7 miles
7 hours

Walk 25

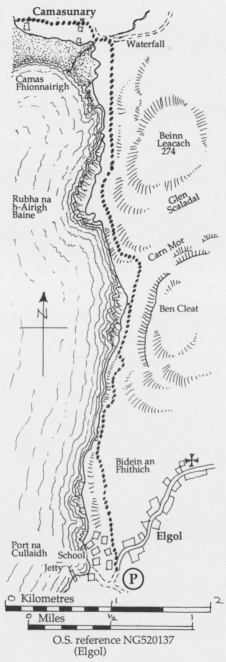

Camasunary

Waterfall

Camas Fhionnairigh

Beinn Leacach 274

Glen Scaladal

Rubha na h-Airigh Baine

Carn Mor

Ben Cleat

Bidein an Fhithich

Elgol

Port na Cullaidh

School

Jetty

P

N

Kilometres

Miles

O.S. reference NG520137
(Elgol)

25. Walk from Elgol to Camasunary Bay

The A881 runs from Broadford to Elgol. It is a narrow road with signposted passing places and takes you through some glorious scenery. The road descends very steeply to Elgol pier at the end of the Strathaird peninsula. Half-way down the hill take the left turn signposted Glasnakille. Just beyond the turn is a large parking area and public toilets. To reach the start of the walk, climb back up the steep incline to a track leading off to the left just before a row of fir trees. This seems very tedious but parking is difficult and you can cheer yourself with the thought that you will be walking downhill on your return.

The walk to Camasunary is magnificent, exhilarating, adventurous and unforgettable. At places the track teeters on the edge of very steep cliffs and some walkers may find their vertigo too much. But walk as much of it as you feel happy about. For all its length one of the loveliest views anywhere in Great Britain lies ahead.

Many children do the walk with their parents; they are naturally nimble and have good balance but there must be no playing with an enormous cliff dropping sheer into the sea at the edge of the narrow path.

Walk along the white pebbled track that leads off to the left. It is bordered with clover, ragwort, vetch, self-heal, knapweed, meadow sweet, yarrow and germander. Just before the white farmhouse,

Yarrow

bear to the right of the fence following signpost directions for Loch Coruisk. Beyond the gate, which needs to be climbed, the track continues straight ahead through bracken. Beyond the next gate, the grassy path continues nearer to the edge of the cliffs, with views ahead of Camasunary Bay.

Once you have crossed a burn coming down from the slopes of Ben Cleat, the path moves right out to the cliff edge, with heather-clad slopes dropping to black rocks below where the sea comes splashing in. With your eyes so much on the path ahead, you will notice the lovely vegetation where ferns, bog myrtle, eyebright, lousewort, orchis and white flax flourish. Occasionally hazels, willow and birches grow precariously on the edge of the path and you can stand and enjoy the view across Loch Scavaig to the Cuillin Hills ahead. To the right lies the fissured bulk of Bla Bheinn, with Marsco beyond, and even further away Glamaig stands palely catching the sunlight. Behind Sgurr na Stri, Sgurr nan Gillean and its satellite pinnacles rear up. To the left lie the pinnacled and peaked Black Cuillin. To your left the island of Soay floats on a grey-blue sea. As you traverse the path, the glorious mountains ahead change colour from black to grey, from grey to blue. Today they are free of mist but the sun does not shine on them and they appear dark and mysterious.

Gradually the path begins to descend into Glen Scaladal, a quiet valley with a wide beach. Here an enormous amount of refuse from boats has been washed up and scars this lovely corner. Cross the bay and climb a muddy path that ascends the cliff opposite just above the top of the shingle. Above, a narrow path begins to climb the slopes of Beinn Leacach. This, too, hugs the cliff edge and passes through some luxuriant vegetation. Where it begins its descent towards Camasunary, look for the row of aspens that thrives on the cliff slope.

If both these narrow paths are very wet and slippery, or the wind increases and makes walking difficult, follow the sheep tracks over the tops of Ben Cleat and Beinn Leacach. Much of the way is over rough mountain grass but the views are splendid and it is exhilarating to find your own way over the moorland with the lovely bay ahead as a guide. Gradually all paths lead down to the turf-edged beach. Cross the tumbling burn by boulders or, if it is in spate, walk upstream to the bridge that carries the cart-track that comes over from the Elgol road.

Cross the springy turf of Camasunary Bay and sit by Abhainn Camas Fhionnairigh. The stepping stones and the shingle spits are under water and you cannot go any further.

This is a wonderful walk for enjoying the sea birds. Gannets dive for fish and lesser black-backed gulls wing their way over the water far below. Shags fly close to the surface and a family of eiders snooze and sleep on the quiet waters of the bay. Sandpipers call and fly and sit on rocks. This walk is nine miles, and takes between four and five hours.

9 miles
5 hours

26. Walk to Camasunary Bay and Loch na Crèitheach from the Elgol Road

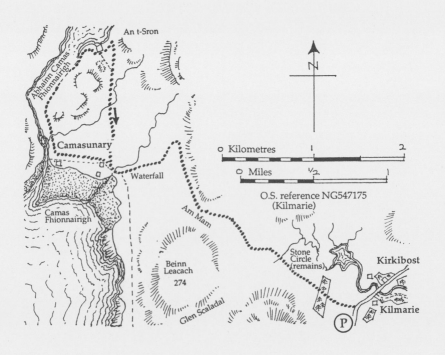

Leave the A850 at Broadford and drive along the A881 single-track road towards Elgol. This takes you round much of Loch

Slapin, with dramatic sea and mountain views. Once past Strathaird House, begin to climb the hill beyond to Kilmarie; half-way up there is a small parking area off the road. It is close to the stile that gives access to the cart-track over the hills to Camasunary. If you have to park on the verges, take care as these can be very soft.

The cart-track climbs steadily and passes through moorland where juncus and buttercups grow. Whinchats sit on a fence and 'chack-chack'. Below to the right, on a heathery hillock overlooking a small dam, several standing stones, remnants of a stone circle, can be seen. Follow the track through a narrow plantation of conifers. Here goldcrests flit, moth-like, among the dead lower branches that overhang the path, quite fearless of passers-by.

Milkwort

The path now swings up through the moorland where the woolly seed heads of cotton grass catch the breeze, and spearwort, lousewort and milkwort grow among the bog myrtle. To the right is the tip of Slat Bheinn. Cross the shallow burn on convenient rocks and climb beside the noisy stream as it races below willow and rowan, passing some pretty falls as it tumbles down the steepish slope.

The track generally is rock-strewn for most of its length but occasionally a grassy area is soft to one's feet and sometimes it is possible to see cobbles. Tormentil edges the track and sundew, growing in the damper areas, is now in delicate white flower. As you continue to climb, the jagged top of Bla Bheinn becomes visible behind the less dramatic Slat Bheinn. When the flattish area at the top of the track is attained, look back to the views across Loch

Spearwort, lousewort

Slapin and Loch Eishort to Sleat. Ahead you have your first glimpse of Loch Scavaig and beyond the imposing bulk of Sgurr na Stri are the Cuillin peaks with their heads in thick cloud. To the right is the jagged side view of Bla Bheinn.

Walk on a few steps and far below lies the wide bay of Camasunary. Gentle white-topped waves come rolling in over the grey-yellow sand, where a large flock of oystercatchers probe for cockles or worms and pipe their clear ringing calls. Continue down the zig-zag in the rocky track, where orchis grow and small voles scurry into the long grass. Overhead a pair of kestrels are quartering the slopes for food for their young – the sun catching the warm brown feathers of the male and turning them almost to gold.

As you descend, crossing a flat wooden bridge over a white-topped foaming burn, the smell of the sea assails you, the sight of the sea inspires you and the quiet mountain fastness fills you with peace. To the south, Rhum seems to float on a sparkling sea. Follow the narrow track across the close-cropped grass in the direction of Loch Coruisk as directed by the signpost. You pass a mountain bothy with a notice on the door – 'Come in to eat your food but take your rubbish out'.

Continue to the edge of Abhainn Camas Fhionnairigh, which flows fast out to sea. On the bank lies all that is left of a bridge, washed away when the river was very high. If you wish to continue the walk to The Bad Step and Loch Coruisk you will have to wade across. But, if the current is too fast and the water too deep, walk up beside the racing burn. The path is a little wet in places but comes after half a mile to the bottom of the lovely falls at the foot of Loch na Crèitheach. On a rock in the middle of the foaming water stands a herring gull looking seawards, with pink legs and yellow beak splashed with red. Long-leaved sundew grows among the wet moss and in the boggy pools water lobelia flowers. Follow the indistinct track to the pebble beach on the loch. Here a party of anglers set off in their row-boat to catch sea-trout, untroubled by the wilful wind that picks up spray and tosses it like a veil towards the head of the loch.

Walk across the beach and take the second path leading from the loch to the shore. Ahead are glorious views of the sea and the sun shines warmly on your face. Wheatears and meadow pipits flit ahead as you move towards the bottom of the track descended earlier.

This pleasing six-and-a-half mile walk is an easy one and can be completed in three to four hours.

Gulls   Buzzard   Hoodies

6¹/₂ miles
3¹/₂ hours

27. Walk to the Point of Sleat

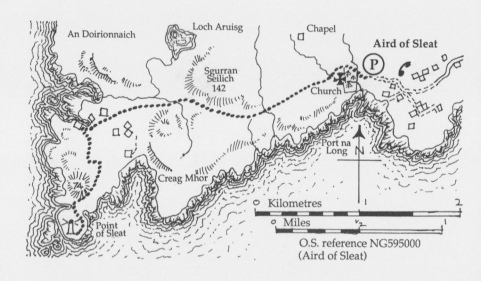

An Doirionnaich

Loch Aruisg

Chapel

Aird of Sleat

Sgurran Seilich 142

Church

Port na Long

Creag Mhor

Point of Sleat

Kilometres

Miles

O.S. reference NG595000
(Aird of Sleat)

Travel by car on the A851 to Ardvasar, and then on the A853
towards the southernmost tip of Skye. The road continues as a
single-track with passing places. The view is magnificent but
the way tortuous and the driver needs to keep his eye on the
road. It can be enjoyed only by passengers. The scenic route
ends at Aird old church, where parking is very limited. Look
for convenient spaces as you approach the end of the metalling
and then walk on to the gate that gives access to the cart-track
beyond. From now on even the driver can enjoy the splendid
views over the sea, to the mainland and the islands.

The good track swings out over the moorland and passes through great banks of ling and heath in full bloom. The verge is bright with devil's bit scabious, lousewort, milkwort, knapweed, tormentil and eyebright. Here an Aberdeen Angus bull strolls among its many cows and calves, looking content and docile, but perhaps it is wisest to make a detour into the myrtle, willow and heather. The heat of the afternoon has brought a swarm of small ants to maturity and the winged insects seem to be everywhere. Grasshoppers 'churr' from the depth of the vegetation, dark brown butterflies flit from plant to plant and a dragonfly darts over the boggy pools. Overhead a pair of buzzards sail and glide, total masters of the air currents.

Look for the dwarf rose trees, some laden with hips, that grow no higher than the heather. Enjoy the ferns that grow luxuriantly wherever there is moisture and shelter. The path begins to climb and when you reach the brow ahead, look back at the lovely views and to a glorious bay below. A pair of peregrines fly overhead. They court and almost touch as they twist, dive and glide like dancers through the air. The path, paved with cobbles on the way down the other side of the brow, gives evidence that this must have been a well-used highway to the old church for the people who once lived in the now ruined and deserted crofts of the settlement ahead.

To the left Creag Mhór looms up, obscuring the view of the sea as you reach a gate. Beyond hurries a narrow, deep, peat-stained burn. It flows through ferns, under rowan and willow where warblers and wrens call, before descending in two waterfalls, one after the other. The lively burn that drains out of Loch Aruisg is crossed twice by plank bridges as it races seawards. After the waterfalls, the burn meanders along a small glen with steep cliffs rearing up on the right. Where it swings away from the path it passes under willow and rowan, and creamy honeysuckle clambers over both.

Honeysuckle

Beyond the next gate, you continue along a narrow path beside which grow beautiful fuchsias sheltered from sea winds by the old walls of the ruined crofts. This was once a substantial settlement but now all that is left are old walls and croft ends softened by willow and scabious, ragwort, wood sage, foxglove and eyebright. Small sessile oaks thrive close to the path.

Pass through the next gate and walk on past a clump of yellow iris bearing large seed pods. Here a whinchat calls from a fence that encloses a planting of mixed saplings. Walk through another gate along a grassy path beside which grows sneezewort yarrow. At the next gate, a written sign directs you to climb by the hinge. When you have done so, pause and look at the tiny harbour, where a man works on his boat.

From now the way onwards is more taxing and the less adventurous may feel they have gone far enough, but it would be a pity to miss the glorious headland. Take care here and turn left. Do not walk down to the harbour. Keep in line with a wire fence that strides uphill. Follow the indistinct and wet path up the heather-clad slopes, keeping close to the fence. Where it turns to the left, follow it down to the valley bottom and then walk to the right, keeping the peat cutting to your right. Make your way uphill, keeping a low slope to your left and a large hill to your right. The way over this shoulder is very wet and you should avoid the parts where cotton grass, sphagnum moss and sundew grow, but once over the top a good path reappears. Follow this to the top of some concrete steps, and, encouraged by the first view of the lighthouse, descend these to a small bay. The path then circumnavigates cliffs and where it is boggy there are stones and driftwood on which to cross the worst.

Beyond the cliffs, cross a narrow spit of land with sea on either side. During high tides and storms this must be under water and the waves have littered it with flotsam. Climb the steps ahead. These lead to a path through the bracken to a grassy sward beyond which is the white-washed concrete ramp to the sturdy white-painted lighthouse. Ascend the ladder to the parapet around the lamp (always alight) and enjoy the

Lighthouse, Point of Sleat

view. Out across the Cuillin Sound lie Rhum and Eigg, hazy in the summer sunshine. Closer inshore and to the south lies the lovely bay, Camas Daraich, where a pair of red-throated divers swim and fish in the clear blue water. Here a heron stands on the twisted and tortured layered rocks, far from the water and from fish. Perhaps it is enjoying the sun. On Eilean Sgorach, an island washed by white breakers, dozens of shags stand with elegant necks curved and bills skywards. Regularly a small group take off and join a large number congregating over a small area of sea that seems to be boiling with a shoal of fish. Gannets fly up the sound and join in the feast, plunging headlong in their spectacular way. To the north-east are the Red and the Black Cuillin, their tops occasionally veiled in mist. To the south-east lie South Morar, Moidart and the Ardnamurchan peninsula.

This is a magnificent climax to a delightful six-mile return walk taking four to five hours. Choose a day when the air is clear, the sun shines and the wind is gentle and you can enjoy the view from the lighthouse and the cliff tops.

28. Walk to Fairy Glen

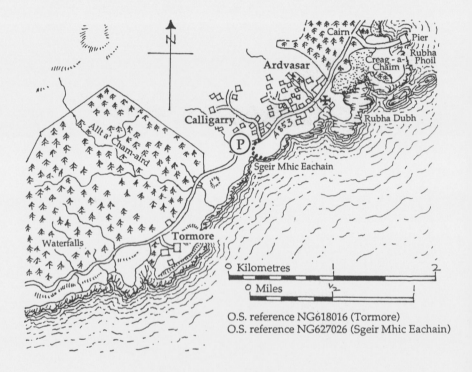

O.S. reference NG618016 (Tormore)
O.S. reference NG627026 (Sgeir Mhic Eachain)

Drive along the A851 past the Armadale Centre and take the right turn for Ardvasar (A853). Drive through the village and park in the road that leads to the settlement of Calligarry. Walk on a few yards along the A853 to a gap in the hedge, just before a bridge over a small burn. By the gap are three steps and a very short track to a gate. The gate gives access to the Fairy Glen that leads to the shore.

A narrow path leads through the glen. Far below hazel, oak and alder, the burn tumbles foam-topped, descending in a glorious waterfall. Where it is joined by a second burn, another spectacular waterfall splashes and sprays below the deciduous vegetation, and under the trees grow ferns.

Follow the narrow path with care because the right side slopes steeply down to the burn. Where the vegetation opens out and you can see the sea, the path follows the curve of the burn and here another delightful fall carries the racing water over the drop in its bed. Where the path enters the bay, hazel, willow, alder, ash and aspen cover the cliffs above.

Along the bank of the burn, just before it enters the sea, monbretia grows and behind this meadow sweet, scabious, bracken, eyebright, valerian and hard fern. In the spring bluebells, primroses and violets cover the banks of the burn. Cross the burn where you can and explore the other side. Look for gipsywort, the pretty skullcap, common hemp nettle growing close to the hurrying water and honeysuckle clambering over tree and bush alike.

Then explore the secret bay at the foot of the Fairy Glen. Sit on the huge rocks covered with barnacles and seaweed and look out to the blue, blue sea between Sleat and the mainland. Perhaps you will see the ferry plying its way to the pier at Armadale, or a yacht tacking towards Mallaig, its white sails billowing. At low tide look in the rock pools for sea anemones, mussels, limpets and coralina seaweed.

The pebbled bay is covered with sea thrift in June and later clover, vetch, silverweed, tom thumb, bog myrtle and wood sage grow where the tide does not reach. Butterflies flit over the flowers and bask on the rocks in the sun. Oystercatchers call from farther along the coast. Terns fly fast and then dive to skim the water for fish, shrieking harshly.

Common vetch

Explore the cleft or grotto at the foot of the cliffs that almost encircle the beach. In the constant spray that falls from above grow luxuriant ferns, willow, aspen, alder and ragged robin.

This half-mile return walk takes you into a secret corner of lovely Sleat. There are glorious views across to the mainland, with its mountain tops veiled in mist.

Ragged robin

¹/₂ mile
1 hour

29. A Walk through the Armadale Centre

Armadale, the Clan Donald Centre, lies five-eighths of a mile from the Mallaig to Armadale ferry. It can also be reached by driving through the Sleat peninsula, using the A851. The ruined Armadale Castle, part of which has now been restored, houses a museum of the Isles and an audio-visual display of the history of the Clan Donald. The castle lies at the heart of the 46-acre grounds, which include mature woodland, pastures, moorland, a farmhouse, a gamekeeper's cottage and more. On a bright sunny day the views are breathtaking. Even on a rainy day Armadale is a joy to explore.

Start your walk with a coffee in the restaurant, housed in the recently-restored stable block. Pay your entrance fee, then pass through the white gates into the estate. Follow the track that leads to the front of the ruin and peer through the gaping windows, imagining what life was like when it was the home of the Macdonalds. Cross the extensive lawn in front of the building; a hill was removed from here so that the owners could enjoy the view. Now you can sit by a stone wall and look out over the Sound of Sleat.

Nature trails through the grounds are way-marked and there are explanations on small notice boards. A leaflet gives a detailed description of the grounds and things to look for. Way-mark 1 is just north-east of the ruin. Here the path passes through rhododendrons. At the start of the walk, look to the right to an iron gate with a double arch now totally overcome by a prolific bush. Pass beneath beech trees (Way-mark 2) where, among moss growing on their boles, flourishes a fascinating lichen called *Lobaria pulmonaria*, now wet and bright green. Look for marbling lichen on the bark of the rowan.

At Way-mark 3 there is a white gate to the road. The trail leaflet suggests you cross the road to look at rock formations on the shore. Here, too, you might see divers, shags and terns. A tern drops a fish it has caught, then catches it before it has dropped back into the sea. A heron fishes quietly in the still waters at the foot of the rocks until a pair of herring gulls chase it away, the heron complaining harshly. Look across the still waters to Loch Hourn to the far left and Loch Nevis opposite.

Return to the white gate and climb the slope through magnificent beech trees. Dog lichen grows among the moss on the bottom of the trunks. Look through the trees for glimpses of the sea and the mainland beyond. Way-mark 4 takes you into a quarry where rock for building work on the castle was obtained. Look for the toadstool garden at the top of the rock face. Through the trees nearby fly a pair of mistles followed by an overlarge youngster.

Try not to miss Way-marks 5 and 6 (on a small loop between 4 and 7) to see the volcanic dyke and, in late spring, the mass of spotted orchis. The narrow path continues with pastures full of sheep and cows on the left and the sea to the right. Where steps lead down to a burn wood avens grow. Beyond the hurrying water, look for trees damaged by roe deer. Look, too, for the jew's ear fungus growing on the elderberry trees; in the rain these become soft and ear-like, but when the air is dry they become black blobs (another reason for walking in the rain!). The larch trees nearby are festooned with *Usnea* – a lichen of pale green feathery tufts as pretty as Christmas-tree decorations.

Way-mark 10 is a gully down which flowed water to power a cornmill near the shore. Beyond is a track to the shore. Turn left and pass through a deer gate and follow a wide track that was the old road. On the left alders and birch lean over the burn and through the trees troop a flock of coal tits. Goldcrests come so close that you can see the chrome yellow on their

Armadale farm

heads and a tree-creeper ascends the bark of an old tree trunk, revealing its presence by its boyish whistle and flashes of its pearly breast.

Continue uphill, looking back regularly to enjoy the views of the bay. Along this path you will meet some splendid rams with curled horns. By the next gate is a seat to pause awhile and enjoy the peace and seclusion. Beyond the gate the track leads to a working farm. Several of the buildings are now disused but how splendid it must have been once. Walk round the front of the building and follow the path as it leads to Waymark 15, where there is a delightful view of the castle, snug in its hollow among the trees.

If the weather is good for views, walk on through the conifers to the gate in the deer fence, which gives access to the heather moorland. Look for the mill dam on the right and then continue to the top of the hill ahead to see the Outer Hebrides and the Cuillin. Return to the path, continuing from Way-mark 15 and walk on through delightful wooded parkland. Here you might disturb a buzzard, which rises from a feast and heads off over the tree-tops. The path, muddy after rain, leads to the game-keeper's cottage now, sadly, deteriorating rapidly. Beside the building are the iron cages, which were kennels for his dogs.

The path leads from the cottage down a dark, slippery path through both conifers and deciduous trees, crossing over the reinforced farm-track and on to the castle grounds. Here, if you are wet and perhaps a little chilly or hot and very thirsty, turn right and head for the restaurant once more.

This three-and-three-quarter-mile walk takes three hours of steady walking – much longer if you are enjoying the mosses, lichens, fungi, birds, trees and flowers, all of which thrive in great abundance in this balmy southern corner of Skye, tempered so gently by the Gulf Stream. Much of the way is easy walking but if there has been rain, boots are the best footwear. You will in Skye, of course, have your waterproofs.

If you still have the energy and some time to spare, cross the road to a 'Footpath to Darnen' sign opposite the centre. Turn right and follow the path to where it forks. Turn left down some steps. After winding among trees on the shore you suddenly come to a rocky outcrop with Scots pines, a seat and an open view of Armadale pier and all the mountains across the sound.

3³/₄ miles

3 hours

30. Walk to Dalavil Wood and Deserted Village

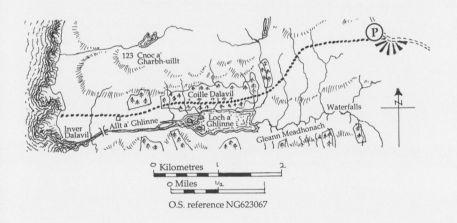

O.S. reference NG623067

This is an exhilarating walk. There is no obvious path, but it is a walk that can be attempted by the old and the young, suitably equipped and with a willingness to explore and to venture. The O.S. Map shows no footpath to Dalavil.

Leave the A851 at the single-track road signposted Achnacloich, four-fifths of a mile beyond Kilmore. Drive for a mile and a half and park in a lay-by that has a signboard saying Clan Donald Lands Trust. Walk down the slope, keeping to the left of the telegraph pole, and continue across the moorland walking through bog myrtle, heather, thyme, self-heal, sundew, milkwort, tormentil, devil's bit scabious and eyebright. Head for large patches of bracken on the slope in

115

the distance, crossing intervening streams by following sheep-tracks that lead you to a suitably narrow place. On reaching the bracken, keep just above it, picking up a good sheep-track. Look around here for the remains of old crofts from which the tenants were moved in the 19th century.

Follow the sheep-track, waiting for the magical moment when you first see Loch a' Ghlinne and the sea beyond, both sparkling and silvery in the afternoon sun. Overhead a pair of buzzards wheel

Self-heal

and soar. Voles and shrews dive into their minute tunnels in the long grass as we pass and dark brown butterflies flutter in all directions.

The track continues and descends diagonally very, very slowly for just over a mile. It crosses several streams, each time at a convenient point. These hurrying small burns are lined with birch, hazel and rowan, the latter heavy with berries and leaves already tinged with red. Beneath the trees grow ferns, wood sage, small rose trees and liverworts. To the left, at the head of the loch, is another ruined croft with its chimney still intact. The loch is an extensive stretch of water, much of it colonised with white water lilies and great reed. Here fish leap. A heron flies over the water calling raucously and then heads off for the sea.

The sheep-track then leads into Dalavil wood, where there is a wider and probably ancient track. To the left, Scots pines lean elegantly towards the loch and beneath them grow many rowan seedlings. Beyond the conifers, the track passes between numerous mature beech trees, many blown down in gales. Here, in the deep moss covering the roots, tiny beech seedlings attempt to grow. Moss also clothes much of the trunks of these splendid trees. The floor of the wood is deep in bronze leaves of last year. Coal tits and young willow warblers call from the trees. Deer roam the undergrowth beyond, leaving their footprints in the muddy track.

Coal tit

Follow the track as it moves out of the wood well beyond the end of the loch. To the left, across a wide grassy tract of land, lies the canal built to drain the land and carry the water from the loch out to sea. The track continues beside a ruined wall and keeps just above the wide and damp hinterland of the canal. It leads to another ruined croft and the remains of others that formed the settlement of Dalavil.

From here walk along the track for five or six yards and then take an indistinct path to the right that skirts the higher ground to the north. This is the path that leads to the beach. Keep along it until you reach a heather-clad outcrop, one of many, above the shore. Stand and enjoy the second magical moment of the walk – when the Inver Dalavil lies at your feet. Here gentle waves lap the many small islands across the bay. On these sit oystercatchers, curlews and greater black-backed gulls. To the right lie the Red Cuillin bathed in sunshine and the Black covered in cloud. Soay lies misty across the placid waters. To the left stretch small cliffs and tiny rocky inlets. Seemingly far out lie the islands of Rhum and Eigg. It is a wonderful reward for the walker who has made the four-mile trek – and still has the four-mile walk back.

8 miles
4 hours

31. Walk to Dunscaith Castle, An Acarsaid Garden and Knock Castle

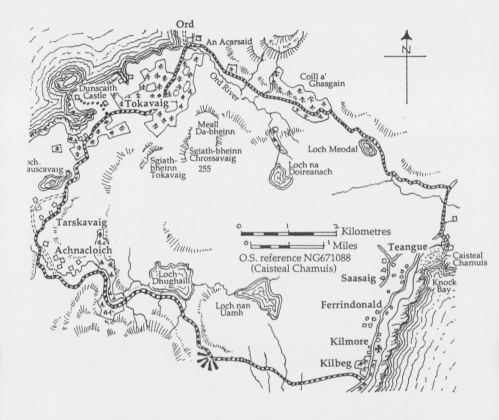

Achnacloich, Tarskavaig, Tokavaig, Ord, Teangue; all delightful names from the Sleat peninsula. Dunscaith Castle is near Tokavaig, An Acarsaid is at Ord and Knock Castle lies close to

Teangue. To see all these, drive along the A851 and take the right turn signposted Achnacloich, four-fifths of a mile after Kilmore.

The single-track road climbs steadily uphill passing through moorland then, as it begins to descend, it passes Loch Dhùghaill and through deciduous woodland that crowds around Gillean Burn. Here grow willow, birch, alder, rowan, hazel and oak. Overhead a pair of buzzards 'keen' and soar. As you continue along the tiny road you pass the scattered settlements of Achnacloich and Tarskavaig. Beyond lies Loch Gauscavaig, a tranquil stretch of water where a solitary great northern diver leaps upward before it makes its neat header into the water.

Drive on and park on the firm ground of Gauscavaig Bay. From here there is an excellent view of Dunscaith Castle

Dunscaith Castle

119

overlooking the mouth of Loch Eishort. Enjoy the views of the Red Cuillin (the Black is in cloud), and enjoy the quietness broken only by the gentle lapping of the tide and the haunting calls of curlews. Look at the outcrops of rock where dog lichen and English stone crop grow.

Curlew

Move on to the end of the bay and park on the firm turf just before the cattle grid and the bridge over the Allt Tokavaig. Walk on and take a turning to the left – a private track where parking is not allowed. When you come almost to the croft at the end of the track, bear left and follow one of the various narrow, grassy paths, where sea pinks grow, leading to the castle ruins. Until late in the 16th century this castle was the home of the Macdonalds. All that is left are two arches that, probably, once supported a drawbridge. It spanned a ravine that connected the mainland with the isolated rock on which the fortification stands. Beyond the arches a row of stone steps leads up to the few remaining walls. Sit on the rocks in the ravine and look out to the island where shags, looking like heraldic eagles, sit with wings outspread to dry.

Return to the car and drive on through the woods beyond Tokavaig, and down the steep slope before crossing the River Ord. Park on the solid grassy shore in front of the entrance to the gardens of An Acarsaid. These are open every afternoon, except Sunday. Voluntary contributions go to the Royal National Lifeboat Association. It is suggested that you follow the red arrows as you move around. What you see is sheer delight. Just how did anyone collect so many similar-sized pebbles to use for mosaic paths, walls, courtyard and steps? Follow the arrows so that you do not miss even one vista. Arrows 8 and 9 direct

Sea pink

you to a viewpoint overlooking Loch Eishort with its backdrop of the Cuillin. Here the owner has kindly painted the silhouette and labelled each mountain. You can see a wide colourful rainbow as the sun shines through a shower out on the loch.

The plants, many of which are unusual, also delight you as you stroll along the paths. What a magical corner this is, in this quiet bay.

From here walk up the hill and take the left turn at the top of the slope. This is a metalled track that leads past Ord House. Continue along the road until you reach a cart-track leading off to the right. Follow this as it swings along the headland and then drops down through grassy slopes. Keep well to the right of the dwelling and walk down to the beach, crossing the little burn that swings in front of the house. Here is a large patch of coral beach formed from calcified seaweed and shells. In the loch a large island has a coral beach that seems to have its own built-in sunlight. Where the coral strand stretches out into the sea, the water above turns to turquoise. On the island itself brilliant green grass grows on a huge boulder. On the next island dozens of seals bask in the sun among the soft warm seaweed below high-tide level. At the far end of the beach, an indistinct path leads up on the headland and continues to the point. Inland the limestone tops of Sgiath-bheinn an Uird shine bright white in the afternoon sun.

When you can drag yourself away, return to the car and continue along the road until you regain the A851. Turn right and drive the half-mile to the farm at Knock, parking in the wide track leading down to the jetty. Walk past the huge barn built round a courtyard that once was the farm steading of the Macdonalds – now, sadly, losing slates and struts. Cross the bridge over the fast-flowing peat-stained beck and continue to the metal gate across the farm-track. Walk a short distance across the grassy verge to a small wooden gate that gives access to a track beneath alders laden with fruit. The burn crossed earlier flows beside the track and through the trees pass an excited flock of long-tailed tits.

Follow the little path past a boat-house on one side and, on the other, large grassy islands in the burn, where a grey wagtail hunts insects. From here you walk up a slope to the remains of Castle Camus, a fortress belonging to the Macdonalds, once defended against the MacLeods. Though only fragments of walls remain, the mystery and magic of the site seem all around it.

Look out to the Sound of Sleat where you might see the yacht Britannia, with the Queen and Prince Philip aboard, guarded by a modern-day fortress – a frigate almost lost in the misty greyness of the waters.

32. Ferry from Sconser to Raasay and Forest Walk

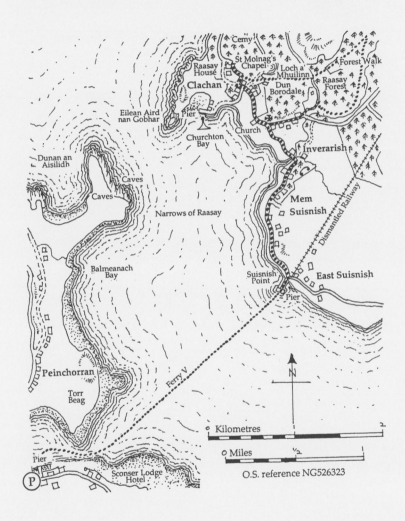

Cemy
St Molnag's Chapel
Raasay House
Clachan
Loch a' Mhuilinn
Forest Walk
Dun Borodale
Raasay Forest
Eilean Aird nan Gobhar
Pier
Churchton Bay
Church
Inverarish
Dunan an Aisilidh
Caves
Caves
Narrows of Raasay
Mem Suisnish
Dismantled Railway
Balmeanach Bay
Suisnish Point
East Suisnish
Pier
Peinchorran
Torr Beag
Ferry
N
Kilometres
Miles
O.S. reference NG526323
Pier
P
Sconser Lodge Hotel

Petrel

Park in the small area reserved for cars by the well-signposted Raasay ferry pier at Sconser on Loch Sligachan. The 15-minute crossing is a delight, with glorious views of Trotternish to the north and the views behind of the mountains of Minginish becoming ever more spectacular as the small car and pedestrian ferry crosses the Narrows of Raasay. As the ferry curves round the shallows of Rubh' an Tòrra Mhóir, look for the shags sitting on the spit of shingle and the oystercatchers crowding closer together as the tide reduces the standing room. A pair of petrels with long narrow blue-back wings fly swiftly and buoyantly ahead of the ferry. Over towards Loch Ainort a storm blots out all colour but a wide-banded rainbow compensates for the greyness of the scene.

Disembark at East Suisnish pier and turn left, walking the one-and-a-half miles to Inverarish. Refreshing sea smells assail you as you walk and the magnificent views can be savoured all along this narrow coastal road. Sandpipers call from the shore and gulls fly across the choppy narrows. Take the left fork, signposted Raasay Hotel, and walk on past it (unless you need a coffee) to the outbuildings of Raasay House. Look at the ancient clocktower whose clock has not told the time for many a day. Continue on and walk into the grounds of the Raasay outdoor centre. This was once the home of a junior branch of the MacLeods and though now rather neglected it must have been a splendid house.

Return to the road and walk on a few more yards to the ruins of St Molnag's Chapel, where many old and not so old tombstones bear witness to the longevity of some families and the sad loss of many young children. Here in the roofless chapel, with sycamores, ash, elm and rhododendrons, is perfect peace.

Walk back along the road and take a footpath behind the outbuildings and clocktower to join a metalled road that rises gently between banks of rhododendrons. After 100 yards, the road passes through conifers alive with goldcrests to the side of charming Loch a' Mhuilinn. In a tall conifer on the opposite bank a heron nests. Huge rhododendron bushes clothe the banks and small islands of the loch. Above the rhododendrons Forestry Commission trees stretch up the mountain slopes and above the trees are rocky outcrops and heather where red deer roam. Turn right and walk beside the loch. To the left, at the far side, is a picnic table set in the trees overlooking the dark peat-stained water.

Continue on along a glorious forest ride between rows of conifer trees, and where the track divides take the right fork named Church Walk. Here on the right of the path tree-like

St. Molnag's Chapel,
Raasay

rhododendrons grow overhead, touching the firs on the other side and turning the path into a shadowy tunnel. The ground is deep in needles, making it soft and silent to walk on. Follow the red signs to The Broch. These direct you through the trees and up a small slope to a delectable clearing where pink and white foxgloves flower and English stonecrop grows in the crevices between the boulders. The Broch, a circular defensive structure, no doubt once overlooked fertile farming land but now lies in a sunfilled hollow deep in the forest. It is a litter of stones, still retaining, after hundreds of years, its original round shape.

Return through the trees and walk on along Church Walk to a large clearing in the forest where there is a house and the free church.

Beyond, the walk once more continues through conifers where large purple-capped toadstools grow. At the gate take the second left, following the signpost direction beyond the bridge for Inverarish. Fifty yards brings you to four long rows of houses that compose the village. These were built in the 1914-1918 war to house German prisoners who worked in the now defunct iron-ore mines. Except for the straightness of the rows of cosy houses nothing now reminds you of how they came to be built.

At the end of the long rows, turn left and walk back along the shore road to the ferry.

Raasay is a tranquil island where the clock seems to have been put back 20 years or more. A visit to it on the ferry, followed by a round walk of six or seven miles, is a delightful way to spend a day if you have walked very hard for several days.

7 miles
4 hours

33. Walk along Loch Sligachan from the Hotel to Peinchorran

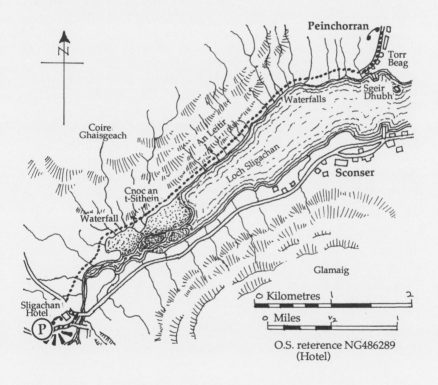

O.S. reference NG486289
(Hotel)

Park behind the Sligachan Hotel and walk round in front of it. Cross the A850 to Portree and walk through the camp-site to a track much used by pony trekkers. This runs along the shore of the loch above the flotsam left by the tide. The track, wet in places at first, leads you through heather and bracken to the Allt Dubh, which is crossed by convenient stones. Walk on, crossing several more streams, one bordered by some interesting basalt rocks. Anglers fish in the loch and sheep feed on the nourishing turf.

In spring sea thrift spangles the shore and in high summer tormentil and marsh bedstraw thrive, with the pretty lousewort growing in the damper areas. Oystercatchers crowd on the exposed spits and fill the air with their restless piping. Ringed plovers, keeping close together, feed and move as one.

A glorious waterfall, crossed by boulders, comes tumbling from the slopes above. You can cross all the streams and burns in good weather, but you would be unable to continue when the rivers are in spate. On another spit a flock of curlews probe and then, when disturbed, fly off down the estuary, their liquid bubbling calls echoing from the lower slopes of Glamaig, the conical mountain overtowering the loch. A flock of green plovers, feeding on the tidal flats, rise with broad, round wings flapping slowly.

From now on there is a better path that moves up above the shoreline below Ben Lee. A red-throated diver swims with its youngster and further out a group of divers feed, sinking rapidly below the water and then just as quickly returning to the surface. Continue along the three-mile path, crossing the many bisecting streams and passing the fish farm out in the loch. The bracken on the slopes is tinged with yellow. From a frond chides an angry wren. Several shags fly down the loch, perhaps to join those that sit on the spit of land, Rubh' an Tòrra Mhóir, round which the Raasay ferry swings on coming into Sconser.

After crossing the Allt Garbh Mor, the path gradually ascends the slope before arriving at Peinchorran. From here there are views across to Raasay and to the 1,456-foot hill of Dun Caan with its flat summit. This is a good path to use when the wind is blowing quite strongly from the sea. Slightly lower down the slopes, several narrow paths take you back to the cluster of houses. These run along the edge of the low cliffs from which you can see the Raasay Ferry plying back and forth. Look on these slopes for the delicate felwort, which grows among the heather, crowberry, eyebright and tormentil.

Crowberry

This is a grand walk for enjoying the waders and sea birds. Choose a day or time, when the traffic making the journey along the opposite side of the loch, below Glamaig, is light because even the sound of the smallest car travels over the water – doubly so having rebounded off the base of the mountain. It is an exciting walk on a blustery day when the wind and the sea birds are all you can hear.

On the return walk you have both the Red and Black Cuillin ahead, with the mysterious Sligachan Glen disappearing into the distance. Or you might prefer to catch the 1 p.m. bus from Peinchorran back to Portree, with spectacular views from the B883 of the mountains of Trotternish.

7 miles
5 hours

34. Walk from Sligachan to Loch Coruisk

Kilometres
Miles
O.S. reference NG486298
(Hotel)

This is a 15-mile hard walk requiring good boots, waterproofs, sufficient food and plenty to drink. It is an expedition for the strong walker and is best attempted when there are long hours of daylight.

Park in the large lay-by on the south side of the A850, close to the Sligachan Hotel. Walk to the old bridge ahead and follow the signposted path in the direction of Loch Coruisk. The path through Glen Sligachan is very wet for most of the way, but there is always a diversion that can be taken round the muddiest areas and convenient boulders to cross the small burns that tumble down the hillside to join the River Sligachan.

Much of the way has cairns, which do help the walker to find the driest tracks.

As you start along the path, look down into the tree-lined ravine through which flows the lovely Allt Dairich. On the little hillock to the right of the path, shepherds meet with their dogs and discuss a hundred or so sheep that they have rounded up from the mountain slopes. A pair of ravens fly across the glen from Glamaig to Sgurr nan Gillean and a sandpiper calls from its reach of the river.

After nearly two miles the Allt na Measarroch is reached. Walk down towards the river until an area of shingle enables you to cross the hurrying water more easily. Continue on below the slopes of Marsco, which hides the dark forbidding bulk of Bla Bheinn. To the right of the path Sgurr nan Gillean rears up into the clouds and a rain storm seems trapped in Harta Corrie beyond. Below the corrie lies Lochan Dubha – a bright china-blue patch among the green foliage of the moorland.

Heather, bog asphodel, bog myrtle and tormentil grow among the coarse moorland grass. Meadow pipits and wheatears flit across the path from heather clump to heather clump and their calls and the constant splashing of tiny streams are the only sounds to be heard in this deserted, secluded glen.

The path divides below Ruadh Stac, the left-hand fork leading down to Camasunary and the right to Loch Coruisk. The latter leads down to the edge of a narrow, fast-flowing burn that is easy to cross on rocks. From here the path at first ascends steadily. Far below you can see an enticing corner of Loch an Athain, with a solitary fisherman in a boat stationary on the green water. Then the path climbs steeply and in sharp zig-zags to Druim Hain. The path is rock-strewn and generally dry – a great relief after the wetness earlier. Look for the sundew growing among

Sundew

131

the sphagnum and club-mosses by the edge of the track. Sit by the cairn at the top and enjoy the view and then walk to the right to a rocky outcrop to see Sgurr nan Gillean and its attendant peaks, a breathtaking view now that the clouds have rolled away.

A path going off to the left leads to Sgurr Hain, but avoid this and begin the long, and at times wet, 1,000-foot descent to Loch Coruisk. On the way down, pause and enjoy the small lochan – Loch a' Choire Riabhaich – with its waterfall below. Keep on down the path, savouring the extensive views over the open sea to Soay and Rhum. Towards the shore of Coruisk, the rocks are waymarked in red and these lead to stepping stones across to the other shore. One row of stones leads to a small island and another to the other side. Look for these boulders at the end of the loch just before the short Scavaig river descends in its spectacular waterfall. Sometimes these stones are under water and you are unable to cross. But hopefully you will be able to reach the opposite shore.

Sit on the great whalebacks of rock and look back to Loch Coruisk and its little islands, where common gulls breed and terns fly overhead, revealing their long slim wings and forked tails. Occasionally one of the gulls comes close – fed by earlier walkers no doubt – and reveals its pale yellowish-green legs and bill. Look up at the great mass of the Cuillin slashed with white as many rivulets race down the sheer sides. In the sea waters of Loch na Cuilce, a little boat negotiates the islands. It comes right into the natural harbour and ties up at the

Sea-gulls

small jetty, where several tourists come on land for a short stay. Walk round into the little bay.

This taxing walk brings you to an especial corner of Skye, perhaps the loveliest. Spend as much time as you can in this secluded sun-trap but do not forget the very long and very hard seven-and-a-half miles back – a trek that can take up to four hours to cover.

15 miles
8 hours

Walks 35 and 36

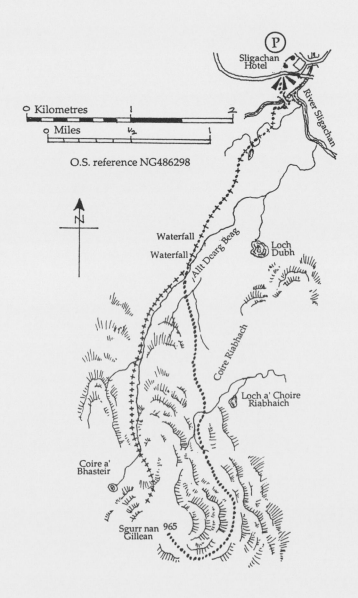

Kilometres

Miles

O.S. reference NG486298

Sligachan Hotel

River Sligachan

Waterfall

Waterfall

Allt Dearg Beag

Loch Dubh

Coire Riabhach

Loch a' Choire Riabhaich

Coire a' Bhasteir

Sgurr nan Gillean 965

35. Walk to the South-east Ridge of Sgurr nan Gillean

When most of the Cuillin are topped in mist, Gillean seems to be clearer. It is the black-pointed spire that overlooks Glen Sligachan. The route described is called the tourist route and for the first part of the way it is just that, but from the ridge onwards it is a pinnacle to be climbed by those with a good

Sgurr nan Gillean

head for heights and nimble of foot. If you suffer from vertigo, you should stay on the ridge and enjoy, vicariously, the pleasures of others ascending the very rough and seemingly almost vertical terrain between you and the top. This is a walk for boots and waterproofs.

Leave the car park at the back of the Sligachan Hotel. Fifty yards along the Dunvegan Road take a footpath to the left. Walk across the peat and heather moorland using a track that is sometimes cobbled and has solid planks across several peat-stained streams. This leads to what was once a power house, but where now only a few brick pillars remain, and a narrow wooden bridge with a hand-rail across the Allt Dearg Mór. The fast-flowing burn is divided by a massive rock buttress. It descends in foaming tresses before placidly flowing over its wide rock-strewn bed, then joins the River Sligachan on its way to empty its water into the loch.

Walk upstream following the well-defined path and then continue along it as it meanders across the heather moorland where young meadow pipits call. The path takes the walker beside a lochan where bogbean flowered earlier and spearwort pushes pretty yellow flowers above the surface. It crosses several very wet areas but someone has placed convenient boulders and it is possible to keep dry.

Bogbean

The path brings you close to the Allt Dearg Béag and to another lovely waterfall where the tempestuous burn descends in two elegant falls into a turquoise pool surrounded by ferns and heather. A rowan grows on the bank and a small row of aspens, their leaves quivering in the slight breeze. The pool is deep but can be entered by a 'beach' and must be ideal for a summer swim.

Walk upstream beside this charming burn to yet another grand waterfall, a perfect subject for the camera, with the pinnacles of Gillean directly above the streaming water.

Just beyond the fall is a narrow plank bridge and the path continues on the other side until a cairn overlooking Coire Riabhach is reached. From here there are magnificent views; backwards towards the Old Man of Storr and to the odd-shaped stack mountain Dun Caan on Raasay; forwards to a necklace of lochans, Loch á Choire Riabhaich, Lochan Dubha and Loch an Athain; and sideways to the peaks of Glamaig, Marsco and Bla Bheinn.

This may be the point for some walkers to start their two-mile return. The more adventurous can follow the narrow, indistinct but reasonably well-cairned path into the corrie, and then begin the zig-zag course up the steep slope ahead. This is at first quite easy but then becomes more difficult, traversing very loose stone. Once the top is reached, the way towards Sgurr Beag continues in an easier manner – for 250 yards! Enjoy the ground-hugging alpine vegetation as you ascend. Look for rock whitlow grass, rose-root, and violets with pretty-shaped capsules full of seeds. Here grow common wild thyme and wild thyme, the latter smelling so much the stronger. See also both the club-mosses, northern bedstraw, green-white cladonia and *Antennaria dioica*, for which there seems to be only a Latin name.

Following the cairns, you then ascend a rocky chute between cliffs, which brings you to an enormous rock field. You traverse this moving steeply upwards all the time, by short sections of grassy patches between vast areas of boulders, until you attain the south-east ridge. Most walkers will venture no further but sit here and watch intrepid youngsters continue upwards, with the terrain dropping sharply away on either side into Lota Corrie on the west and to equally sheer slopes on the east. When they believe they have reached the summit, the way drops down for nine yards only to rise again to the true summit.

From your viewing platform, with your back tucked safely against a rock, notice the climbers on the nearby pinnacles and listen to their conversations across the abysses between. They disturb the mountain silence so much that a raven flies around the top croaking angrily.

This is a grand eight-mile trek (nine to the summit) – walk for as long as you are able and enjoying the rewards of your effort! It takes six to seven hours.

Swallow

8¹/₂ miles
6¹/₂ hours

36. Walk from Sligachan to Coire a' Bhàsteir

Park in the large lay-by behind the Sligachan Hotel. Here a stoat races like a furry pencil across the tarmac. Cross the Dunvegan Road and take either of the tracks that lead across the moorland to the bridge over the Allt Dearg Mór. Both paths are well used and both are muddy in places, but earlier walkers have placed stones that enable you to cross dry-shod and making good use of these adds to the exhilaration of the walk.

Stoat

Once over the cascading burn, follow the path that takes you safely across the wet moorland. Do not hurry this part. Always look ahead for the best way over or round a boggy patch. Enjoy the small lochan to the left of the path covered with bogbean. After a mile across the moor, where heather and bog myrtle grow and meadow pipits call sweetly, you come to the edge of the Allt Dearg Béag, your companion – and a very delightful one – for the rest of the walk.

Walk upstream, dawdling beside the spectacular waterfalls where the river descends between heather and fern shaded by small aspens, birch and rowan, the latter laden with fruit in late August. Continue upwards passing the plank bridge over the racing burn. (This is the place to cross the burn if you are intending to walk on towards Sgurr nan Gillean.) The Allt

Dearg Béag comes down in great haste, a deep turquoise river that foams and sparkles as it races over its rocky bed. In spate it rages and boils but it can be a gentle burn, and then you can sit on the huge rocks and enjoy your sandwiches.

Pause on the climb and look across the moorland to Portree, to the Storr mountains, to the Old Man himself and to Dùn Caan on Raasay. The way up to the Coire is now cairned, easy to follow and not arduous, but it does climb relentlessly. As you ascend, notice how all the small rivers that drain the mountain slopes above eventually unite and swell the Allt Dearg Béag. As the path enters Coire a' Bhàsteir, look for alpine lady's mantle growing in large clumps covered with pale lemon flowers. Both club-mosses grow close to the path and wild thyme thrives between the boulders. Much of the Coire is covered with boulders and scree and most ways up to the tops above are over this difficult terrain. Walk over to the left of the Coire and look up the gorge to the depths of the mountain fastness. Look out from the Coire to the far distance. Portree is now lost to sight in a storm but beyond the rain you can see both the Storr and Quiraing.

Coire a' Bhàsteir

This is an exciting five-mile walk and one that can be undertaken by old and young. It takes you into the heart of a mountain revealing a great, barren, rocky wilderness. Time taken, three to four hours.

5 miles
3¹/₂ hours

37. Walk through the Forest, South-west of Portree

Leave Portree by the A850 Broadford to Kyleakin road. Half a mile along the road, look for the cemetery on the left and, just beyond it, the entrance to the Forestry Commission's car park for the forest walk. Look through the few trees screening the park to the still waters of Loch Portree and the houses on the other side. From the trees behind the park come the sweet whisperings of goldcrests.

Pass through the kissing-gate in the corner signposted 'Forest walk' and climb the narrow path beyond. Willow, rowan and alder

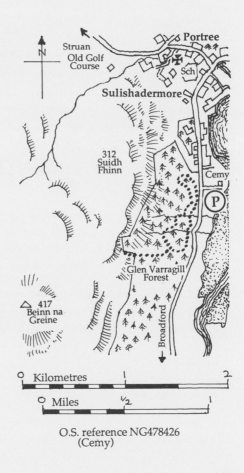

O.S. reference NG478426 (Cemy)

border the path but behind them serried rows of conifers stretch on and on. Below the deciduous trees water avens flourish in June. The path, way-marked in white, leads to an open area between compartments of the forest and crosses a little burn racing pell-mell downhill. Enjoy the wild raspberries growing on either side of the path among bracken, heather, hardheads, devil's bit scabious, meadow sweet, tormentil, marsh thistle and valerian.

Marsh thistle

Follow the path as it moves in among the trees, where much of the light is excluded. Occasionally a gap in the canopy allows wood sorrel leaves to flourish among a deep carpet of moss. Trailing threads of moss cover some of the lower branches of many of the trees. As the path ascends you walk along its zig-zags to a small clearing and then to a wide unmetalled forest road. Look for dog lichen just beginning to colonise the sloping edge of the road.

Turn left as the way-mark decrees and walk along the road. Look for the huge boletus and the red and white toadstools that grow beneath the firs. Through the trees a goldcrest, quite unafraid of the walker, flits from branch to branch. Walk on along the road to where, on the left, a narrow path starts the descent to the road – but do not descend. Instead ascend the narrow grassy fire break, on the right, that climbs the steep slope towards Beinn na Greine. After rain this can be very muddy and it is better to move into the trees and climb keeping parallel to the ride. Beneath the trees the ground, cushioned with thick soft moss and a deep layer of needles, is a joy to walk.

Along the ride honeysuckle, bog myrtle and self-heal flourish and coal tits 'si, si, si' quietly from the conifers. At the end of the ride the trees on the right continue up the slope sheltering a large clearing of heather and bracken. A small family of robins come close, hopping on the ground and on low growing branches near our feet. One of the parent birds scolds from close by and occasionally utters the start of its poignant song. From the top of the fire break you can see the waters of the loch.

Return through the ride to cross the forest road, continuing downhill along the narrow way-marked path. Just before it swings to the left, look for orange-peel fungus growing on the bare soil. Follow the path as it comes to a railed area overlooking a clearing in the forest with views across the loch. Move on along the viewing area and look down on the tranquil harbour with fine mountains behind.

Follow the way-marks carefully downhill. The indistinct path passes through dense forest where little light penetrates. It then widens and drops steeply where mist drifts between the trees below you. The path now keeps close to a chuckling stream until a clearing is reached and the burn is crossed by a bridge. Here there is a seat for a quiet rest.

The way-marks then direct you through another flower-filled clearing before entering the trees once more. Overhead a buzzard calls eerily. And then the path comes close to the road and you walk within sound of the traffic to the car park.

This is an excellent two-mile walk taking an hour or more. Enjoy the scent of the conifers, the colour of the summer flowers in the clearings, the views from the high point and from the viewpoint and the quietness and the seclusion.

2 miles
1 hour

Buzzard